CFA Institute

FINANCIAL REPORTING DISCLOSURES

Investor Perspectives on Transparency, Trust, and Volume

CFA Institute is the global association of investment professionals that sets the standard for professional excellence. We are a champion for ethical behavior in investment markets and a respected source of knowledge in the global financial community.

Our mission is to lead the investment profession globally by promoting the highest standards of ethics, education, and professional excellence for the ultimate benefit of society.

ISBN 978-0-938367-76-5
July 2013

Contents

Foreword

Disclosures provided in connection with financial statements are essential to an investor's understanding and analysis of the economics underlying the information in financial statements. Because of the importance of disclosures to analysts and investors, CFA Institute—which is composed of such professionals—undertook a study to provide investor views on the effectiveness of financial reporting disclosures. Consideration of disclosure reform from the investor perspective is an important contribution that had yet to be included in a substantial way in the current dialogue on disclosure effectiveness.

This report, which is only one element of the study, provides results from a survey that sought investor insights into developing a disclosure framework specifically and enhancing the effectiveness of financial disclosures generally. Also included in this report are recommendations to improve overall disclosure effectiveness based on more than 40 years of CFA Institute's liaising with investors and commenting on financial reporting matters on behalf of our members specifically and investors in general.

We would like to extend thanks to members of the CFA Institute Corporate Disclosure Policy Council, who reviewed and provided input to this report.

Executive Summary

Initiatives are under way to reform financial reporting disclosures. The current dialogue is centered on developing a disclosure framework—an overarching framework—that will make disclosures more effective. CFA Institute supports enhancements in disclosures because high-quality financial statement disclosures are essential to an investor's understanding and analysis of the economics underlying a company's financial performance and such understanding is fundamental to sound investment decision making.

As we describe in Section 1, we believe that disclosure reform proposals should focus principally on meeting the information needs of investors, who are the principal consumers of financial statement information. We also provide background on the importance of disclosures to investors along with CFA Institute's historical perspectives regarding the principles of high-quality financial reporting and disclosures.

As we reviewed contributions to the disclosure reform initiatives currently in progress—and experienced the dialogue on disclosure reform—we noted that such efforts were heavily informed by reports based on interviews, surveys, and the work of preparers, accountants, and auditors rather than investors. As would be expected, the conclusion of such research is that investors are inundated with excessive financial statement disclosures and, therefore, may overlook the most relevant financial information. The ensuing inference is that disclosure reform should principally aim to reduce the quantity of disclosures.

Because investors are the consumers of financial reporting and disclosures and their input is an important contribution yet to be made in a substantial way to the dialogue on disclosure effectiveness and reform, CFA Institute believed it was important to leverage our membership (analysts and investors using financial statements)—and our four decades' worth of experience in liaising with investors on financial reporting matters—to provide investor perspectives on disclosure reform.

We conducted a survey of our members in 2012 (Appendix A provides details of the 2012 Disclosure Survey). Based on the findings of this survey, prior CFA Institute surveys, and our longstanding relationship with the investment community, we developed this report to provide investor views on disclosure reform priorities and provide recommendations to enhance financial reporting effectiveness.

Disclosure Reform: Consider in Context of Investor Experiences and Current Environment

Missing from the discourse on disclosure reform is, in our view, consideration of how recent economic events and secular trends have informed policymaker efforts to reform financial reporting disclosures. Investors believe that any dialogue regarding financial reporting and disclosure reform must be informed by current events and the current environment, or context, into which such reforms might be introduced. Without such a frame of reference, it is not possible to ascertain whether such reforms will be effective at addressing sources of disclosure ineffectiveness.

Further, if financial reporting is meant to serve the needs of investors, it only seems appropriate that current disclosure reform initiatives give consideration to investors' present frame of reference and the lens through which investors evaluate disclosure effectiveness. To that end, Section 2 provides background on the events and factors currently shaping investor perspectives.

Financial Crisis: Inadequate Disclosures Contribute to Lack of Transparency, Trust, and Investment

Investors' perceptions regarding financial reporting effectiveness have been profoundly affected by how they experienced the events leading up to, during, and following the 2008 financial crisis. How well disclosures served their needs during this tumultuous period unequivocally informs their views regarding the efficacy of financial reporting and disclosures.

Investors believe the 2008 financial crisis—and the ensuing five years of economic uneasiness—plainly revealed the insufficiency of disclosures, especially those of financial institutions. Investors point to the countless reporting and analyses of high-profile financial institution failures and bailouts during, and since, the 2008 financial crisis as evidence of the insufficiency of disclosures in providing the necessary transparency to investors regarding exposures, risks, uncertainties, and leverage of such financial institutions.

This lack of transparency in financial reporting—especially when it occurs in financial institutions—leads to loss of investor trust and, in turn, the reluctance of investors to invest. Without trust in financial institutions—the handmaiden to the broader economy—there is an ensuing lack of investment in the broader economy. Recent commentary by laymen, sophisticated investors, and regulators demonstrates the lack of investor trust emanating from the lack of transparency in disclosures. Excerpts of such commentary are included in Section 2 because such remarks exemplify what CFA Institute has heard repeatedly over the last five years from our members and investors regarding the overall lack of transparency in financial reporting and the ensuing lack of trust and lack of investment in the broader economy.

Investors, informed by such recent economic events, find it surprising that disclosure reform efforts currently under way—after the greatest financial crisis since the Great Depression and during a period of continued economic uncertainty—have concentrated on reducing disclosures instead of improving the disclosures that proved most troublesome, thereby enhancing transparency and, ultimately, trust for investors. The paradox grows when investors contrast current efforts with policymakers' responses to the Great Depression, which led to the Securities Act of 1933 and the Securities Exchange Act of 1934, both resulting in an enormous expansion in disclosures.

Five years after the 2008 financial crisis, it is difficult to point investors to anything substantial that has been done other than consolidating certain off-balance-sheet vehicles (a project under way prior to the crisis), addressing limited repurchase agreement abuses, and adding certain credit risk disclosures. Illustrative of the point is that the financial instruments project remains incomplete.

Disclosure reform proposals need to establish a link to how they will improve the disclosures investors found most problematic during the financial crisis (e.g., undisclosed risks, judgments, and estimates; off-balance-sheet items; and going concern issues). Investor confidence that standard setters are working to increase transparency reestablishes confidence in financial markets and, correspondingly, a willingness of investors to invest that will lead to a normalization of markets.

Other Key Factors Affecting the Current Financial Reporting Environment

While it is important for standard setters and policymakers to consider financial reporting and disclosure reforms in the context of recent investor experiences, it is also important for them to consider other matters investors perceive as impacting the current financial reporting environment. These matters include the following:

- *emerging trends in technology and connectivity,*
- *the inability of the existing accounting model to provide investors with sufficient decision-useful information in a new economy, and*
- *the lack of a measurement framework that can inform the disclosures necessary to make such measurements meaningful.*

These are all factors that influence the usefulness of financial reporting and disclosures for investors. Yet these influences are absent from the conversation regarding how best to reform disclosures. We explore each of these in more detail in Section 2 because we believe they should shape policymakers' thinking.

Investor Priorities: Enhancing Elements of Transparency and Quality

The 2012 Disclosure Survey asked CFA Institute members to prioritize a variety of potential financial reporting initiatives in order to ascertain what they believed should be the focus of standard setters and policymakers in their efforts to improve financial reporting and disclosures. What is poignantly illustrated in **Figure 1**, and discussed in further detail in Section 3, is that what investors believe should be the focus of standard setters' efforts (left side of chart) is diametrically opposed to where standard setters are currently focusing their efforts (right side of chart).

As noted in Section 3, investors also believe—when specifically asked the question—that improvements in financial statement presentation should be addressed before developing a disclosure framework.

Disclosure Framework: Efforts and Objectives

The Financial Accounting Standards Board and the European Financial Reporting Advisory Group are developing, or exploring the possibility of developing, a disclosure framework to make financial statement disclosures more effective and coordinated and less redundant. The International Accounting Standards Board has also started a short-term initiative to explore opportunities to improve and simplify disclosures.

As can be seen in Figure 1, investors tell CFA Institute that the development of a disclosure framework is not a top priority for them. Because it has been an area of standard setter focus, we asked members for their perspectives on the specifics of this initiative. Key findings are articulated in Section 4 and summarized here:

- Investors support a disclosure framework designed to guide disclosures, but

Figure 1. Investor Priorities vs. Standard Setter Focus

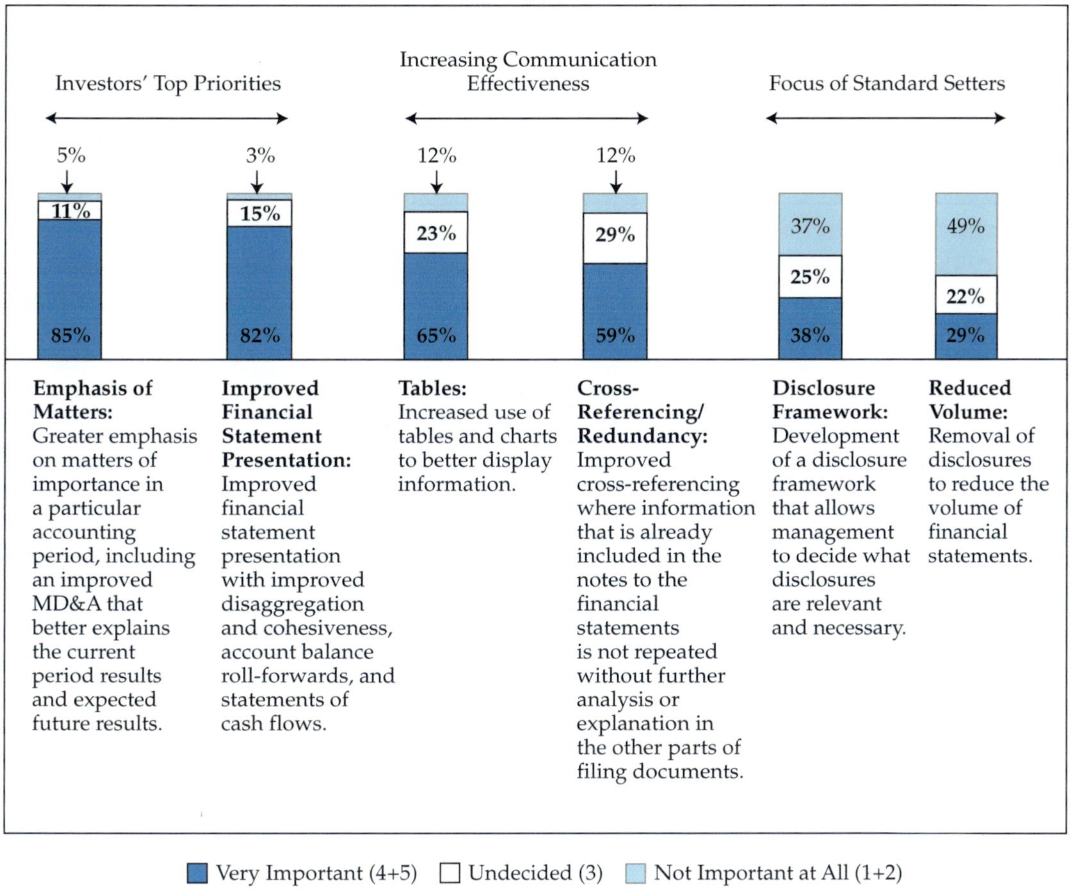

Notes: The question was, How important would each of the following potential financial reporting changes be to you in the use of financial statements? As for responses, $N = 303$.

- they believe that specific disclosure requirements in the individual accounting standards should be retained and the disclosure framework should complement, not replace, existing disclosure requirements; and
- investors consider increasing the effectiveness of disclosures, better integrating information, and emphasizing matters of importance the primary objectives of a disclosure framework project.

Investor Concern: Not Volume but Completeness of Information

Given the recent focus on enhancing disclosures principally through a reduction in quantity, we asked members whether the volume of disclosures is an area of investor concern. Section 5 notes that 80% of respondents indicated that volume is not a significant financial reporting concern. This finding is consistent with the response others receive from sophisticated investors; however, it is a finding not well publicized. Members also rejected recommendations on ways to reduce disclosure volume by excluding certain information, such as accounting policy footnotes and other publicly available information. Respondents cited concerns over the need for comprehensiveness, the dynamic nature of information sources, how a complete set of financial statements would be defined, and the cost to investors of collecting such information as their major objections.

Many preparers, pointing out the growth of annual reports, posit that they contain excessive information without considering whether the information provided is complete. Investors do not equate disclosure volume with complete and comprehensive information. Instead, they note the disclosure shortcomings evidenced during the 2008 financial crisis and wonder what is being done to ensure that disclosures address these shortcomings and afford greater transparency. In Section 5, we consider further whether volume equates to completeness of disclosures.

The results of our work suggest that efforts to reform disclosures should focus on increasing the quality and completeness of disclosures, not reducing the volume of disclosures. Investors neither seek a reduction in disclosures nor believe they can be overloaded with useful information. Additional useful information provides investors greater transparency into their holdings, which has been found to ultimately reduce the cost of capital, as we illustrate from the research cited in Appendix C.

Complexity: A Disclosure Driver, Not a Result of Disclosures

Some suggest that increased disclosure volume has created complexity in financial reporting. As noted in Section 6, however, our experience with investors suggests that volume is not synonymous with complexity. We see three key sources of complexity:

1. complex businesses and transactions,

2. disclosures that do not meet disclosure objectives that result in providing all the information required to understand items recognized and measured in the financial statements, and

3. accounting standards that do not clearly communicate the underlying economics of transactions or that use disclosures to substitute for appropriate recognition, measurement, or presentation.

Increased complexity of businesses, structures, and transactions is driving the need for greater and more robust disclosure requirements. Increased disclosure complexity as a result of increasingly global and complex businesses is something investors will adapt to. Inadequate communication and inadequate accounting standards can, however, compound complexity. These factors need to be mitigated so that increasingly complex activities are clearly conveyed to investors.

Materiality: Where Is All the Immaterial Information?

There has been much discussion and commentary regarding materiality, its definition, and the perception that financial statements are full of immaterial clutter that obscures key messages. As discussed in Section 7, while there have been many such generalized claims, we believe more precise research needs to be done to identify specific examples of inclusion of immaterial information and the basis for its inclusion so as to identify and address its causes. The results of our 2012 Disclosure Survey suggest that the majority (76%) of respondents do not currently observe the inclusion of obviously immaterial information. More specific examples of the inclusion of immaterial information may facilitate reconciliation of differences in perspective.

A dialogue on materiality specifically as it relates to disclosures needs also to consider that materiality judgments are made by heterogeneous groups—preparers, auditors, and users—that are likely to have dissimilar views on materiality thresholds. Research demonstrates that, in general, users have lower materiality thresholds. Therefore, we recommend, first, aligning the definitions of materiality found in various pieces of the accounting, audit, and regulatory literature in such a way that the investor perspective is central to the definition. Second, we recommend that materiality judgments exercised by preparers and auditors be disclosed. This would enable users to more easily assess the materiality of information in the financial statements.

Recommendations: Enhancing Financial Reporting and Disclosure Effectiveness

As previously stated—and as illustrated in **Exhibit 2**—it is important to consider investors' views on financial reporting and disclosure recommendations in the context of factors investors perceive as affecting the current financial reporting environment. The 2012 Disclosure Survey and our outreach to investors show that the most effective way to enhance transparency would be for standard setters to prioritize certain financial reporting improvements ahead of establishing a disclosure framework. We have provided recommendations in the following areas, in order of importance to investors:

1. *Financial statement presentation.* Investors believe improved financial statement presentation is a key element to improving financial reporting because poor financial statement presentation limits transparency. Disclosures are less effective when the financial statements that are the foundation they are meant to complement are not effective or when disclosures are meant to compensate for poor presentation. Thus, we provide recommendations (1–4) related to enhancing financial statement presentation.

2. *Communication and presentational enhancements.* Our survey reveals the need for enhancements in communication style and presentational changes to make information more digestible and effective in communicating the company's results. These areas are common ground for investors and preparers. To this end, we provide recommendations (5–10) of this nature.

3. *Most troublesome disclosures.* The 2008 financial crisis highlighted disclosures that our previous surveys, as set forth in Appendix B, identified as causing the greatest problems for investors. Therefore, we reiterate the importance of improving disclosures in these areas before, or as a part of, the development of a disclosure framework. Furthermore, to truly explain the economic substance of transactions and events, preparers and auditors should go beyond requirements if necessary. See recommendations 11–17.

We have also addressed matters for consideration (18–21) by standard setters in any decision-making process to improve disclosures. Considerations such as materiality, technology, effective cost–benefit analyses, and evaluation of the underlying behavioral elements that lead to disclosure problems are important for standard setters to incorporate in their decision-making processes.

Finally, we have also included specific elements (22–27) for consideration in the development of a disclosure framework.

Exhibit 2 provides a summary of the context and recommendations that are described in detail in Section 8.

Exhibit 2. Recommendations Based on Factors Affecting Investor Views on Current Financial Reporting and Disclosure Environment

A. Factors

Financial Crisis/Great Recession:
Lack of Transparency → Lack of Investor Trust → Lack of Investment

Technology:
The Irreversible Trend toward Greater Connectivity and Data in Financial Reporting

Existing Accounting Model:
Providing Decision-Useful Information in the New Economy?

Measurement:
Resolving Measurement and the Disclosures That Make Measurements Meaningful

B. Recommendations

Financial Statement Presentation	Communication and Presentational Enhancements	Most Troublesome Disclosures	Considerations to Incorporate in Decisions to Improve Disclosures	Considerations Specific to the Development of a Disclosure Framework
1. Disaggregation	5. Integration	11. Estimates, judgments, and choices	18. Materiality	22. Focus on equity investors
2. Direct method cash flow statement	6. Entity-specific information	12. Risks	19. Technology	23. Include disclosure objectives
3. Cohesiveness	7. Emphasizing matters of importance	13. Off-balance-sheet items	20. Costs and benefits	24. Maintain specific disclosure standards
4. Roll-forwards of key balance sheet accounts	8. Organizing and layering information	14. Commitments and contingencies	21. Behavioral elements	25. Disclosures should be a focus, not afterthought, in development of standards
	9. Simple language	15. Intangible assets		26. Comprehensive information source
	10. Tables and charts	16. Going concern issues		27. Applicability (entities and reporting periods)
		17. Go beyond requirements if necessary		

1. Disclosure Focus: Investors

CFA Institute's financial reporting policy positions, including our views on the importance of financial disclosures, were documented in our 2007 publication titled *A Comprehensive Business Reporting Model* (*CBRM*).[1] The *CBRM* is a financial reporting framework that articulates 12 core principles that should govern financial reporting.[2] The *CBRM* is based on our earlier publication titled "Financial Reporting in the 1990s and Beyond" and on advocacy efforts spanning more than four decades.[3]

The *CBRM* articulates our views on disclosures as follows:

> Corporate financial statements and their related disclosures are fundamental to sound investment decision making. The well-being of the world's financial markets, and of the millions of investors who entrust their financial present and future to those markets, depends directly on the information financial statements and disclosures provide. *Consequently, the quality of the information drives global financial markets.* (p. 1)
>
> Investors depend on financial information for their investment decision making. For example, investors routinely use financial disclosures in evaluating a company's growth prospects, its riskiness, and the long-term success of the company's business model. These analyses also provide the inputs investors need to price individual securities and to make portfolio decisions. Taken altogether, the quality of investors' pricing and capital allocation decisions affects the relative efficiency and effectiveness of financial markets. Simply put, *when financial disclosures do not tell the economic story as it really is, the prices of securities, and even the amounts of capital allocated to a company, are less likely to reflect the company's actual economic position*. (p. 11)[4]

The global investment community requires high-quality, comprehensive information to be able to understand and properly evaluate the quality of reported earnings, the changes in the equity of a company, cash flows, and other financial statement metrics. This information is

[1]CFA Institute, *A Comprehensive Business Reporting Model* (Charlottesville, VA: CFA Institute, 2007): www.cfapubs.org/toc/ccb/2007/2007/6.

[2]*CBRM* (pp. 56–59).

[3]"Financial Reporting in the 1990s and Beyond" (1992). A summary of this report may be found in the *Financial Analysts Journal*, vol. 48, no. 6 (November/December 1992):21–23.

[4]Unless otherwise noted, italics in quoted material indicate emphasis added by us.

needed to appraise company performance and understand the company's wealth-generating processes. Common shareowners and potential investors use the information to make forecasts of future cash flows, evaluate the sustainability of the company's business model, and assess its cash-generating ability. This information, in turn, is used to estimate the investment's value and future changes in such value.

To provide users with this information, the financial statements must recognize, as they occur, all events or transactions that affect the value of the company's net assets and, hence, common shareowners' wealth. Financial statements cannot be fully understood, however, without extensive, clear, and complete supporting disclosures.

Principle 12 of the *CBRM*, Effective Disclosures, states that the role of disclosure is to provide a full explanation of events or transactions that have been recognized in the financial statements, their measurement properties, and their risk exposures. This includes (1) the models, estimates, assumptions, and principles that were applied to measure the events and transactions and (2) the sensitivity of the reported information to changes in those principles and assumptions. To the extent that financial statement line items present aggregated information, disclosures must enable investors to disaggregate.

Disclosures Are Not a Substitute for Recognition

Disclosures are meant to complement, not substitute for, balance sheet and income statement recognition and measurement decisions, and they are essential if investors are to understand the financial statements. The following quotation sardonically conveys this point:

> So, if you tied up your neighbor and robbed his house, but you disclosed it in Footnote No. 23, it's okay.[5]

[5]Howard Schilit, forensic accountant and author of *Financial Shenanigans: How to Detect Accounting Gimmicks & Fraud in Financial Reports*, quoted in "A Financial Sleuth Finds a World of Abuses," *Barron's* (31 March 2012).

Disclosures Should Not Be an Afterthought for Standard Setters

Because financial statements and their associated disclosures go hand in hand, disclosures should also not be mere postscripts to recognition and measurement in the standard-setting process or in the preparation of financial statements. CFA Institute has commented for decades that there is too little focus on disclosure requirements and that efforts related to developing disclosures occur too late in the standard-setting process. Proposed standards that exemplify this issue include revenue recognition, leases, impairment, and insurance. Disclosures are the means by which the recognition and measurement principles are communicated. Without disclosure being an effective communication device, the effects of recognition and measurement principles on financial statements cannot be understood by investors.

Disclosures Should Be Company Specific and Prepared with Rigor Equal to That Applied to Basic Financial Statements

Because disclosures are an essential and indispensable complement to the financial statements, the same qualitative characteristics of financial reporting—including understandability, completeness, relevance, and comparability—apply equally to disclosures as to financial statements. The information and measurements contained in disclosures should not be any less reliable than that which is recognized in the financial statements and should be subject to the same level of audit scrutiny. In addition, these disclosures should pertain to the individual characteristics and circumstances of the company involved. That is, they need to be entity specific in order to be meaningful to investors.

Disclosure Focus Should Be to Provide Useful Information for Equity Investors

To elicit the objective of disclosure reform, we must first consider the objective of financial reporting itself. Principle 1 of the *CBRM*, Information Needed by Suppliers of Capital, states that the primary objective of financial reporting is to meet the information needs of equity investors, creditors, and other suppliers of risk capital so that they can make their resource allocation decisions.

Furthermore, Principle 2, Perspective of Equity Investors, states that primacy must be given to the needs of equity investors over the other suppliers of risk capital. Existing common shareholders are the residual claimants on the net assets of a company. All other claims are senior to their claims. As stated in the *CBRM*,

> Financial statements should serve the needs of all those who provide capital to a company and bear risk as a result, including the various classes of creditors as well as equity owners. However, among all classes of capital providers, common shareowners are the residual risk bearers in a company. Hence, we believe that one of the *primary objectives of financial reporting and disclosure must be to provide all of the information that owners of common equity require to evaluate their investments*. (p. 5)

Residual claimants need complete information about the business, its risks, and other claims on the entity's cash flows in order to value their own investments. Given that the residual risk bearers require the most complete information regarding all claims, we believe that if their information needs are met, then the needs of those with senior claims will also be met.

Because disclosure reform should be focused principally on meeting the information needs of equity investors, those who are developing disclosure reform proposals must ask the investor community the following:

- how they perceive current financial disclosure information,
- whether current disclosure requirements and financial reporting disclosures meet their information needs, and
- what changes they believe are necessary to increase transparency in disclosures for investors.

Need for Investors to Weigh In: CFA Institute's Call to Action

The important and indispensable role of financial reporting disclosures and the need for investor input regarding disclosure effectiveness served as a call to action for CFA Institute to ascertain investor perspectives on these issues and, on that basis, how best to effect disclosure reform.

In order to do this, we conducted a survey of CFA Institute members in 2012, which we will refer to as the 2012 Disclosure Survey.[6] The survey results are highlighted in various sections of this report. We found that the themes emerging from the 2012 Disclosure Survey are consistent with messages we have obtained from previous CFA Institute surveys.[7]

We believe it is essential that the voice of the investor be heard in the process of developing disclosure reform. In the next section, we explore the context that informs investors' perspectives and the lens through which disclosure reform proposals will be viewed by investors.

[6]Background on the approach and methods of the 2012 Disclosure Survey and information on the geography, occupations, and experience of respondents are presented in Appendix A.
[7]Previous surveys are summarized in Appendix B.

2. Disclosure Reform: Consider in Context of Investor Experiences and Current Environment

Investors believe that a conversation regarding financial reporting and disclosure reform should occur in the context of recent economic events and secular trends and how they have been experienced and perceived by investors. These events and trends should inform the policy response.

Policy Response Should Be Informed by Recent Events

As Benjamin Graham and David Dodd highlighted in 1934 on the first page of the first edition of their seminal work, *Security Analysis,*

> Any present examination into financial principles or methods must *start with a recognition of the distinctive nature of our recent experiences*, and it must *face and answer the numerous new questions which these experiences inspire.*[8]

Graham and Dodd are referring to the need to evaluate finance and investing concepts resulting from the events of 1927–1933 that led to the Great Depression. We suggest that the same line of thinking should be followed when we assess the current state of financial reporting effectiveness.

Investors' perceptions of financial reporting are unequivocally affected by their experiences of the events leading up to, during, and following the 2008 financial crisis. Therefore, the effectiveness of financial reporting disclosures should be evaluated in light of their performance in serving the needs of investors during this tumultuous period. Furthermore, if financial reporting is meant to serve the needs of investors, financial reporting and disclosure reforms should be considered through the lens by which investors see these issues.

[8]Benjamin Graham and David Dodd, *Security Analysis*, 1st ed. (New York: McGraw-Hill, 1934):1.

Historical Context: Great Depression = Securities Acts and Enhanced Transparency in Disclosures

The Great Depression of the 1920s and 1930s led to the adoption of the Securities Act of 1933 and the Securities Exchange Act of 1934 (the Securities Acts, often referred to as the "truth in securities" law) and an enormous expansion of disclosure requirements. The Securities Acts were based on this philosophy of disclosure: The goal of the laws is to require issuers to fully disclose all material information that a reasonable investor would require in order to make up his or her mind about a potential investment. The laws also aim to prohibit deceit, misrepresentations, and other fraud in the sale of securities. That is, the laws seek to increase transparency and trust for investors.

In the first edition of *Security Analysis*, Graham and Dodd make the following observation about the transparency of disclosures—specifically, revenue disclosures—in the period leading up to the passage of the Securities Acts:

> It is unfortunately true that less than half of our important enterprises supply this very moderate quota of information. *Withholding of data—particularly of annual sales—is usually justified on the ground that it might be used by competitors or customers to the detriment of the company and therefore of its stockholders.* Such assertions are rarely convincing, especially since they are contravened by progressive managements in every line of industry. Concealment of the sales total or the depreciation charge severely handicaps the analyst and the intelligent stockholder because it renders impossible any thoroughgoing study of the results. Nor can it be denied that *the restriction of this important information to a small group identified with the management may at times be of great benefit to them and of disadvantage to the general public.* The same is true of the failure to issue reports oftener than once a year.
>
> *If the stockholders of companies pursuing such archaic policies of concealment would bring sufficiently vigorous pressure upon their managements, many changes for the better could speedily be brought about.* (p. 44)

In editions subsequent to the passage of the Securities Acts, Graham and Dodd updated their thinking as follows:

> *Prior to the passage of the Securities and Exchange Act it was unfortunately true that less than half of our industrial corporations supplied this very moderate quota of information.* (By contrast, data relative to railroads and public utilities have

> long been uniformly adequate.) *The S.E.C. regulations now require virtually all this information to be published* in the original registration statement (Form 10) and the succeeding annual reports (Form 10-K). *Quite a number of companies have requested the S.E.C. to keep their sales figures confidential, on the ground that publication would be detrimental to the enterprise. Most of these requests have been either withdrawn or denied.*[9]

We highlight these passages because they reflect the enhanced transparency in financial reporting disclosures brought about by the Securities Acts. The passages demonstrate that policymakers can improve disclosures for the benefit of investors. They also provide a historical context by which investors can evaluate the actions policymakers are currently taking to improve transparency and trust in the markets.

Financial Crisis and Investor Perspectives on Effectiveness of Disclosures: Inadequate Disclosures Contribute to Lack of Transparency, Trust, and Investment

The investor perspective on the effectiveness of disclosures during the recent financial crisis is that inadequate disclosures contributed to lack of transparency, lack of trust, and, in turn, lack of investment.

Investors Point to Examples Illustrating Lack of Disclosure and Transparency

Countless reports and analyses are available of the failures of such firms as Lehman Brothers, MF Global, and Bear Stearns as well as of the enormous losses, bailouts, or acquisitions of such entities as Morgan Stanley, American International Group, Countrywide, and Merrill Lynch. For example, a press release by the Committee on Financial Services of the U.S. Congress dated 14 November 2012 reporting its investigation of the MF Global failure underscores the lack of disclosures made in just this one high-profile case:[10]

---

[9]Benjamin Graham and David Dodd, *Security Analysis*, 6th ed. (New York: McGraw-Hill, 2009):92.

[10]The report title is "Financial Services Oversight and Investigations Subcommittee Report on MF Global."

> Since MF Global *did not initially disclose the full extent of its European bond holdings*, federal regulators and the investing public were not aware of all the risks facing the company.
>
> The belated disclosure in October 2011 of its extensive European RTM portfolio—which amounted to 14 percent of MF Global's total assets—combined with poor earnings news prompted credit rating agencies to downgrade the company's credit rating to junk status.
>
> The downgrade set off a "run on the bank" by MF Global's investors, customers and counterparties that created a liquidity crisis during what would turn out to be the company's final days.

These are U.S. examples, but equally compelling examples of U.K. and European financial institutions that suffered similar fates can be cited. Each illustrates a situation in which corporate managements did not communicate to investors the possible implications and ramifications, under different scenarios, of certain of their business activities and risks.

The lack of transparency has persisted into the postcrisis era. The following examples illustrate that point.

- *International Financial Reporting Standards (IFRS) enforcement in Europe.* Two recent reports issued by the European Securities and Markets Authority (ESMA) highlight the persistence of the lack of transparency in the financial reporting by European institutions, particularly with respect to the risks and uncertainties they face.

  The first report, "Activity Report on IFRS Enforcement in the European Economic Area in 2011," issued in June 2012, states,

  > Companies have continued to face risks to their businesses as a result of the continuing generally unfavorable economic climate. *Within this context, the disclosure of the possible impact of risks and uncertainties faced by the issuers* regarding judgments and estimates used in the preparation of financial information *has gained even more importance.* Nevertheless, *there are still issuers that have not achieved a satisfactory level of transparency, mainly because of their continued use of boiler-plate disclosures rather than attempting to accurately describe facts specific to the issuer and/or transaction.* (p. 15)

The second report, issued by ESMA in July 2012, summarizes its review of a sample of 42 European financial institutions with significant exposures to Greek government bonds. "Review of Greek Government Bonds (GGB) Accounting Practices in the IFRS Financial Statements for the Year Ended 31 December 2011" found that issuers fell short of meeting IFRS disclosure requirements, particularly in relation to transparency of gross exposure, maturities, valuation methodologies, and fair value levels used, as well as the impact of impairment on profit or loss.

- *JPMorgan Chase London Whale trades.* The U.S. Senate recently released a report on the high-profile derivatives losses at JPMorgan Chase in 2012.[11] The report includes an analysis of what those inside JPMorgan Chase knew about the losses compared with what they disclosed publicly to investors. The analysis shows the lack of transparency in the disclosures made to investors both orally and in the financial statements. This report highlights the persistence of transparency issues and underscores for investors that they have a basis for their distrust.

We mention these examples and findings to illustrate that from an investor perspective, a lack of transparency existed, and continues to exist, in financial reporting disclosures—particularly disclosures from financial institutions. Such lack of transparency has implications for investors' trust and their willingness to invest, which we consider more fully in the next section.

Implications of Lack of Transparency: Loss of Investor Trust and Willingness to Invest

The impact of the lack of disclosure transparency on investor trust and willingness to invest may be best demonstrated through recent commentary of investors, securities regulators, and others on the issue.

A Laymen's Explanation of the Issue

A recent article in the *Atlantic*, "What's Inside America's Banks?" does an excellent job of explaining in layman's language the link between the financial crisis and the lack of transparency in bank financial statements, the continuing opacity in bank financial reporting, and the ongoing lack of trust by even sophisticated investors.[12]

[11]U.S. Senate Permanent Subcommittee on Investigations, "JPMorgan Chase Whale Trades: A Case History of Derivatives Risks and Abuses," U.S. Senate (March 2013).
[12]Frank Partnoy and Jesse Eisinger, "What's Inside America's Banks?" *Atlantic* (2 January 2013).

Using the disclosures in Wells Fargo's financial statements, the authors illustrate the connection between disclosures, transparency, and trust. A full reading of the article provides the most comprehensive understanding of the implications of a lack of disclosure transparency for investor trust, but several interesting and illustrative excerpts follow:

> Some four years after the 2008 financial crisis, *public trust in banks is as low as ever. Sophisticated investors describe big banks as "black boxes" that may still be concealing enormous risks*—the sort that could again take down the economy. A close investigation of a supposedly conservative bank's financial records uncovers the reason for these fears—and points the way toward urgent reforms. (p. 1)

> *When we asked Dane Holmes, the head of investor relations at Goldman Sachs, why so few people trust big banks, he told us, "People don't understand the banks," because "there is a lack of transparency."* (Holmes later clarified that he was talking about average people, not the sophisticated investors with whom he interacts on an almost hourly basis.) He is certainly right that few students or plumbers or grandparents truly understand what big banks do anymore. *Ordinary people have lost faith in financial institutions.* That is a big enough problem on its own.... But an even bigger problem has developed—one that more fundamentally threatens the safety of the financial system—and it more squarely involves the sort of big investors with whom Holmes spends much of his time. *More and more, the people in the know don't trust big banks either.* (p. 3)

> *A crisis of trust among investors is insidious. It is far less obvious than a sudden panic, but over time, its damage compounds. It is not a tsunami; it is dry rot.* It creeps in, noticed occasionally and then forgotten. Soon it is a daily fact of life. *Even as the economy begins to come back, the trust crisis saps the recovery's strength.* (p. 5)

A Sophisticated Investor's Perspective on Transparency of Disclosures

Recently, Paul Singer, an investor and hedge fund manager from the investment fund Elliott Associates, had an exchange with Jamie Dimon, CEO of JPMorgan Chase, at the 2013 World Economic Forum.[13] Singer reiterated the views he had previously expressed to his investors regarding the opacity of financial institution reporting and the need for more disclosures and greater transparency. He believes added disclosures and transparency are necessary so that

[13]The complete exchange can be viewed at http://www.weforum.org/sessions/summary/global-financial-context-0, beginning at approximately 15 minutes into the videocast.

we can begin a process of normalizing the financial system. Dimon's response was to quote the number of pages in the JPMorgan Chase Form 10-K, as if the volume of disclosures reflects sufficient transparency in financial reporting—a common preparer view.

The exchange between Singer, Dimon, and the interviewer, Maria Bartiromo, is excerpted (or paraphrased) and summarized here:

> **Singer:** *One doesn't know from disclosures, or one can't find out from disclosures, whether global financial institutions are actually risky or sound,* and I think that is something which needs to be fixed by global cooperation.
>
> **Bartiromo:** Who fixes this? Whose job is that to fix?
>
> **Singer:** Regulators.
>
> **Bartiromo:** Jamie, would you like to jump in?
>
> **Dimon:** With all due respect, Paul, hedge funds are pretty opaque. You've made this comment publicly before. I called you up and asked you what you'd like to know. *You probably have not read our Form 10-K. It is 400 pages long where we break out assets by...*[14]
>
> **Bartiromo:** What about that Paul?
>
> **Singer:** It's great to have the opportunity to continue my conversation with Jamie in this intimate setting. [laughter]
>
> He is right about, in a way, the opacity of hedge funds, but I would remind everyone that no hedge fund supplied any systemic risk in the 2008 crisis. It's for a very specific and important reason. Most of us, almost all of us, in the hedge fund community—though I don't deign to speak for all hedge funds, but I know a little bit about the industry—are customers of organizations like Jamie's.... As

[14]Dimon goes on for several minutes to describe the improvements since the financial crisis and the positive things JPMorgan Chase has done during and since the crisis. The remarks are not replicated here as they are not directly related to Singer's original point. They may be found at the link to the webcast given in the previous footnote.

such, we have credit departments looking over our credit and all of our positions all the time. Jamie, of course, runs one of the most widely respected large financial institutions in the world.

What 2008 showed was that many financial institutions didn't actually have a handle on—nor did their regulators—the nature of their risks and risk models which were being used were not adequate to describe transmission mechanisms. So, I'm not saying in any way that the system or any institution or group of institutions is unsound. All of the things which Jamie said about the risks that they take and the services they provide—as well as his colleagues, of course—is accurate. What I am saying is that *the path to normalization and a crystal clear ability of global financial institutions to exist outside of an implicit governmental guarantee partially is dependent upon more deleveraging and more disclosures.*

And, just one more point in answer to Jamie's question on the kinds of disclosures necessary. *My June report to investors contains a host of disclosures that my team of 150 investment professionals would like to see* because every time I say we have a billion dollars with this firm or two billion dollars with that firm, please tell me chapter and verse of about their financial condition. *After weeks of analysis and discussion, people come in and shrug, and that actually describes the ability of people—outsiders—to understand the financial condition.* So, I'm just making the point that deleveraging, separating trading from the deposit guarantee positions, would be extremely useful in normalizing the global financial system.

A Securities Regulator's Perspective on Transparency and Trust in Markets

In his speech titled "Capital Formation from the Investor's Perspective" at the American Institute of Certified Public Accountants conference on the current developments at the U.S. Securities and Exchange Commission (SEC) and Public Company Accounting Oversight Board (PCAOB) in December 2012, SEC Commissioner Luis Aguilar highlighted the lack of trust among individual investors and the importance of full and fair disclosure in enhancing investment and capital formation. Following are illustrative excerpts from that speech:

One persistent after-effect of the financial crisis has been a loss of confidence in the securities markets among individual investors. A recent survey finds that only 17 percent of Americans trust the stock market. Average daily trades in U.S. stocks are about half their 2008 peak. From 2006 through 2011, U.S. domestic equity funds experienced a total outflow of half a trillion dollars. Some of this shift may be a natural result of the aging population of baby boomers, but there may also be a decline in the willingness of even younger investors to invest in the stock market. Looking back over a longer timeframe, the number of U.S. IPOs fell sharply after the tech bubble burst in 2000 and never truly recovered, particularly in the case of smaller companies with sales of less than $50 million per year.

To the list of factors contributing to the loss of confidence is the recurring news of household names being sued by the SEC for fraudulent behavior, dramatic breakdowns in corporate governance, or other misconduct. It is understandable that *investors feel uneasy. It's hard for them to know whether the capital markets are trustworthy.*

Obviously, we need to turn this trend around. It is clear that *if you want people to invest in the capital markets, you have to foster trust in the capital markets.* And for that to happen, the capital markets must be trustworthy....

My experiences as an SEC Commissioner make it clear to me that rules to *promote full and fair disclosure, reliable financial information, and accountability for market participants are absolutely necessary.* When properly enforced, such rules help to deter fraud, protect investors and enable true capital formation.

Summary of Investor Perspectives on Transparency and Trust

The 2008 financial crisis and the ensuing five years of economic uneasiness that have followed provide innumerable high-profile examples of financial reporting disclosures that were, or continue to be, lacking in transparency. The quotes and citations in this section exemplify what CFA Institute has heard repeatedly over the past five years from our members and investors regarding the overall lack of transparency in financial reporting. Insufficient disclosures and lack of transparency in financial reporting lead to an ensuing lack of trust and lack of investment in the broader economy.

Differences between Investor and Preparer Perspectives

Previous sections highlight investor perspectives on the disclosure dilemma. The perspective of the preparer community is very different. Preparers, pointing to voluminous and ever-growing annual reports, posit that these reports provide sufficient information for investors. Indeed, they suggest, the information provided is excessive and may be detrimental for users because excessive disclosure volume may obscure key messages, causing users to overlook the most important pieces of information in all the clutter. Hence, the belief of the preparer community is that disclosure reform should be focused on reducing the quantity of disclosures—a line of thinking that appears to be shaping standard setters' policy responses to the recent recession. Investors disagree. They believe disclosures were, and continue to be, insufficient.

The lively exchange between Singer and Dimon perfectly encapsulates this difference. Preparers tend to equate the volume of pages in the financial statements with transparency (see Dimon's remarks), whereas investors do not believe the disclosures are sufficient (see Singer's remarks). As Singer points out, investors have a list of additional disclosures they would like to see and the volume of JPMorgan Chase's Form 10-K does not equate to it being sufficiently transparent.

In sum, investors and preparers see the disclosure dilemma, and the necessary policymaking solutions, very differently.

Great Recession Policy Response = Reducing the Volume of Disclosures? Investors See Need to Redefine Policy Response toward Greater Transparency and Trust

Investors find it surprising that the financial reporting and disclosure reform efforts currently under way are more significantly concentrated on reducing the quantity of disclosures instead of improving the information essential to investment analysis and decision making. The paradox grows when investors contrast current efforts—in a period following the most significant financial crisis since the Great Depression and a period of continued economic uncertainty—to the response by policymakers to the Great Depression. At that time, the financial crisis led to substantial reforms in disclosures with the passage of the Securities Acts.

As investors have experienced the dialogue on disclosure reform, there is little mention of or connection between the recent financial crisis and how it informs the need to improve the quality of disclosures. In fact, five years postcrisis, it is difficult to point investors to anything substantial that has been done to improve financial reporting effectiveness other than consolidating certain off-balance-sheet vehicles (a project already under way before the crisis), efforts to address repurchase agreement abuse, and the addition of certain credit risk disclosures, especially when the financial instruments and related liquidity and interest rate risk projects remain incomplete. The protracted debate and the handling of investor input on these two projects have served only to diminish investors' confidence that an investor-focused solution will be achieved. To investors, the recommendations made by the Enhanced

Disclosure Task Force of the Financial Stability Board (FSB) with respect to improving risk disclosures by financial institutions are useful, but these are *recommendations*, not requirements.[15]

Not only does a disclosure reform dialogue focused on reducing the volume of disclosures not address investors' concerns, but it also works to further erode the trust and confidence investors have in companies, markets, and policymakers. Standard setters, regulators, and policymakers need to concern themselves with this matter as they consider how financial reporting effectiveness can be improved so as to normalize financial markets and investing. Disclosure reform proposals need to establish a link to how they will improve the disclosures that investors found the most problematic during the financial crisis. These disclosures relate to undisclosed risks, judgments and estimates, off-balance-sheet items, and going concern issues. Establishing such a connection would increase credibility that regulator and standard setter efforts are working to address investor concerns. Increased transparency will increase public trust in financial reporting, which will, in turn, lead to increased investment and a normalization of markets.

Other Matters Investors See as Influencing the Financial Reporting Environment

Standard setters and policymakers should consider financial reporting and disclosure reforms not only in the context of the recent financial crisis but also in light of other matters investors perceive to be affecting the financial reporting environment. These matters include trends emerging in technology, the ability of the existing accounting model to provide investors with decision-useful information, and the lack of a measurement framework. Although these are not all the factors investors perceive as important, they are matters that have the most direct link to improvements investors currently see as necessary to making financial reporting, in general, and disclosures, specifically, more useful for investors' decision making.

Factors such as the high degree of macroeconomic uncertainty and associated political uncertainty and risks, increasing globalization, expansion of investment outside of the developed economies with sophisticated capital markets, and an increase in complexity of businesses, transactions, and instruments—all bring with them an increased desire for information and financial reporting disclosures. Without sufficient information to understand such risks and uncertainties, and their impact on potential investment opportunities,

[15]Enhanced Disclosure Task Force, "Enhancing the Risk Disclosures of Banks," Financial Stability Board (2012).

investors are unable to appropriately price and make risk-adjusted investment decisions. Although we haven't considered each of these factors separately, we would like to point out the importance for policymakers to remember that global macroeconomic trends will undoubtedly increase the need for disclosures.

Technology: Irreversible Trend toward Greater Connectivity and Data in Financial Reporting

The majority of accounting standards and financial reporting regulations were written before there was a computer on every desktop (circa 1990) and a smartphone in the palm of everyone's hand (circa 2010). Prior to the implementation of EDGAR from 1993 to 1996, financial reports of U.S. public companies were not available without a written request to the issuer to mail a copy. EDGAR helped democratize the availability of financial information. Implementation of data tagging using XBRL in 2009–2012 in the United States was an extension of the financial reporting process by allowing data capture at the end of the process, which makes data more flexible and interactive. Similar advancements have been made in jurisdictions outside the United States.

Certainly, significant enhancements have been, or promise to be, made in the delivery of financial reporting information to the investing public. However, when evaluated in the context of the use of technology and the availability of data in other aspects of our lives and in light of the economy, investors see substantial room for innovation and improvement. Consider, for example, the advancement in mapping and direction technology over the same period of time. We have moved from hard copy maps to smartphones that can provide us directions in seconds. Do the reforms in technology related to financial reporting disclosures seem as sweeping?

Where Is the Discussion of Technology in Enhancing Disclosures?

Investors recognize the implementation of technology elsewhere and see the opportunity for better use of technology in financial reporting. The time is fast approaching when companies (preparers) that say, "We can't provide that information; it's too costly to obtain" will be heard by investors as saying, "We can't manage this business" or "We are unwilling to provide the information." Advances in technology and connectivity in the past five years and talk of "big data" have irreversibly changed expectations regarding the extent to which data are available, the speed by which data can be delivered, and the impact data can have on decision making—including investment decision making. Yet, in the dialogue on disclosure reform, there is little discussion about how technology can be used to improve the quantity, quality, and timeliness of information for investors. Rather, at this very time, when expectations regarding the availability of data are increasing, the conversation on disclosure reform is focused on reducing the volume of disclosures. This irony is not lost on investors.

Investors believe the conversation about disclosures specifically and financial reporting more broadly needs to consider the vast changes in technology that have occurred in the past 10–20 years. The conversation needs to consider how technology can be effectively leveraged to provide the information investors need for investment decision making in a globally connected, data-driven economy. Investors do not seek a reduction in data or volume of disclosures as they have the ability to utilize technology to evaluate the data. Identifying ways to effectively capture, manage, analyze, present, and deliver financial data is the reform investors see as necessary. How technology can be harnessed to reform the financial reporting process end to end—not simply in the filing of documents with regulators as in the case of EDGAR and XBRL—is where investors believe the dialogue on disclosure reform should be focused.

Changes in Technology and Connectivity Need to Be Part of Policymakers' Decision-Making Processes

An excerpt from the "Global Agenda Outlook 2013," published by the World Economic Forum, highlights the new reality that technology imposes on business people and policymakers:

> *The boundaries of physical and digital worlds are melting at unprecedented speeds, leaving many of our policy-makers, heads of government and business people unprepared to integrate new concepts into decision-making processes.* Technologies have evolved and continue to do so, while vast amounts of data are sent and received by billions of interconnected devices. As interdependency grows between individuals and the systems they are a part of, what are the issues and opportunities to be grasped? (p. 16)

Recognition by accounting standard setters and policymakers of the changes in technology (i.e., in connectivity and delivery of data) and the bearing such changes have on the perceived quality and relevance of their decisions is essential for the sustainability and relevance of financial reporting and accounting standard setting in the eyes of investors. Investors believe standard setters and policymakers need to integrate into their decisions the effect changes in technology have, or could have, on capturing, managing, analyzing, presenting, and delivering financial data.

The SEC's 21st Century Disclosure Initiative and 2009 report titled "Toward Greater Transparency: Modernizing the Securities and Exchange Commission's Disclosure System" seeks to incorporate a vision of improved technology in the delivery of investor information. We laud the SEC for these efforts but would like to see greater progress on this front. The SEC's focus, however, is on the method of delivering information or data, not on the nature of the information or data to be delivered. The latter is the responsibility of standard setters. Therefore, we believe standard setters, such as the International Accounting Standards Board (IASB) and the Financial Accounting Standards Board (FASB), need to incorporate advances in technology into their policy-making and standard-setting decision processes. Presently, we do not find that standard setters are incorporating, in a substantial way, consideration of the changes in technology in their recognition, measurement, and disclosure decisions. For example, recent FASB and IASB decisions regarding revenue disclosures under the new revenue recognition project did not appear to incorporate any consideration of how technology could be used to more effectively and efficiently deliver what investors said were highly relevant revenue disclosures. Rather, the decision-making process was framed around how not to require additional costly information. No discussion is discernible of how technology could be leveraged to reduce those perceived costs. If standard setters are going to perform cost–benefit analyses in their decision-making processes, investors believe they should require preparers to provide an assessment of how technology can be leveraged to reduce the perceived costs.

Existing Accounting Model: Providing Decision-Useful Information in Today's Economy?

Like the delivery of financial reporting information, the accounting model that underpins financial reporting was developed more than 40 years ago in an economic context that is significantly different from today's context. Some suggest that while the accounting model is suited for a manufacturing economy, the existing accounting model may not provide the most decision-useful information for today's investors, given that the current economy is heavily based on information technology, financial services, and services generally.

Technology Companies

For example, valuation of intangible assets is important to technology companies in explaining their value to investors, yet there is no reflection of such intangibles in the financial statements or any disclosures in the notes regarding how such values might be assessed. Investors thus question whether financial statements for this segment of the economy provide meaningful and decision-useful financial information.

Financial Institutions

Similarly, standard setters are struggling to establish a standard for the reporting of financial instruments and insurance contracts that will provide meaningful information to investors. The recent financial crisis and the ensuing period when prices for financial institution stocks have traded at amounts substantially below book value per share (i.e., price-to-book ratios below 1.0) have signaled to many investors that the historical cost accounting model has not stood up well in providing decision-useful information on risk-taking businesses, such as banking and insurance. That is, the market is communicating that either reported assets are overvalued or liabilities are understated. Banking and insurance, however, are about making expectations of, and pricing, future risks, yet there is a struggle to develop accounting, reporting, and disclosure models that investors will find useful. Investors need forward-looking measurements (discussed in the next section) and clearer disclosure of the nature of the underlying risks, of the sensitivities of such risks to market fluctuations, and of the development of such risks over time.

Impact on Investors

To the degree that the accounting model has not kept pace with changes in the business environment in which it operates, the model should be modified to remain relevant. An alternative, but less satisfying, solution for investors would be to provide disclosures that can complement a less-than-optimal model. If neither solution is done, a shadow financial reporting environment will become more relevant, and less reliable, to investors than the formal financial reporting environment. To remain sustainably relevant, the accounting model should adapt to the economic forces shaping the underlying businesses.

Resolving Measurement and the Disclosures That Make Measurements Meaningful

For financial reporting to be most relevant to investors, a measurement framework that defines the characteristics of assets and liabilities that determine their basis for measurement in financial statements is essential. The conceptually inconsistent measurement of assets and liabilities currently used in financial statements, at inception and subsequently, limits the usefulness of such information for investors. The inconsistency and noneconomic nature of the measurements make them difficult to use.

Investors generally focus on two key measurements—cash and fair value. They adjust the accounting measurements (which are generally something other than cash or fair value) to the economic measurement (cash or fair value) of their choosing. Accordingly, establishing a measurement framework that uses economically relevant measurements and defines how and why assets and liabilities are measured on such bases would better guide investors to the measurements that are most useful for their analysis and investment decision making.

The Measurement Approach That Supports Decision-Useful Information for Investors

CFA Institute supports the use of fair value measurements. Our support emanates from decades of anecdotal and empirical evidence demonstrating that fair value measurements provide the most decision-useful information for investors. Our support for this measurement approach does not come without a requirement for additional presentation and disclosure enhancements to make fair value disclosures meaningful. The most important requirement to complement fair value measurement is a direct cash flow statement. The use of fair value together with a direct cash flow statement supported by sufficient disaggregation and cohesiveness principles would allow investors to evaluate fair values in the context of the actual cash generated by the enterprise, which is highly decision useful. Disclosures regarding the assumptions used in arriving at fair value measurements and sensitivity analyses of such fair values are also necessary to enhance investors' financial analysis and investment decision-making process.

Forward-Looking Information

Standard setters need to resolve the debate about the inclusion of forward-looking information in financial statements in favor of the inclusion of such information. Forward-looking information is the only decision-useful information for investors. Investing decisions are made looking forward, not backward. Thus, investors are not troubled by the inclusion of forward-looking measurements, such as fair value measurements, if given sufficient disclosure with respect to cash flows, the assumptions made in arriving at the fair value measurements, and the sensitivities of the values.

A common refrain when assets or liabilities are to be measured at fair value—or if there were a requirement to provide disclosures of forward-looking information (e.g., the expected cash flows related to financial assets and liabilities)—is that such information cannot be provided in the financial statements because the information is forward looking. This common refrain fails to recognize that existing accounting standards and financial statements are awash with the use and inclusion of forward-looking information. Examples are the measurement of accrued expenses, percentage-of-completion and program revenue, insurance liabilities, derivatives, equity securities, fixed-maturity securities held for sale, pension obligations, litigation accruals, goodwill, and intangibles. Each measurement requires the use of substantial forward-looking information. As such, this refrain should be considered in the context of the substantial amount of forward-looking information already included in the financial statements.

Investors perceive standard setters to be inconsistent with respect to the inclusion of forward-looking information. For example, standard setters believe fair value information is too forward looking to use in the measurement of loans, but they propose a forward-looking measurement of credit losses. Thus, standard setters need to define what makes some forward-looking information acceptable to include in financial statements and other forward-looking information unacceptable.

Financial Reporting vs. Financial Analysis

Finally, it has been said that the inclusion of forward-looking information such as fair value in the financial statements results in financial analysis being performed within the financial statements. The use of fair value in financial reports does not eliminate the need for financial analysis. Rather, it provides a more relevant basis for financial analysis. Historical cost information, by contrast, provides information that does not facilitate financial analysis as it is not decision useful or relevant to an investing decision being made today.

A Consistent Measurement Framework Can Guide Disclosure

A consistent measurement framework provides a standard context in which disclosures can be provided. A consistent measurement framework could inform more consistent disclosure requirements. For example, an entity measuring a liability at amortized cost in the financial statements would be required to disclose the fair value of the liability, the cash flow characteristics of the liability, and a sensitivity analysis along with related assumptions. Consistent requirements and presentation for each type of measurement would enable investors to more readily identify and use the necessary information.

With this understanding of investor perceptions regarding the effectiveness of disclosures and the current financial reporting environment, the next section explores investor views on how standard setters and policymakers might best bring about financial reporting and disclosure reform.

3. Investor Priorities: Enhancing Elements of Transparency and Quality

As part of the 2012 Disclosure Survey, we asked CFA Institute members to provide their input on the importance of a variety of potential financial reporting and disclosure improvements. The results are summarized in **Figure 1**. Evident from review of the figure is that investors believe the focus of standard setter and policymaker efforts to improve financial reporting and disclosures (left side of figure) is diametrically opposed to where they are currently focusing their efforts (right side of figure).

Members indicate that the financial reporting reforms of highest priority to them are greater emphasis on matters of importance during a reporting period and improved financial statement presentation. This is followed by enhancing communication methods through, for example, increased use of tables and charts and better cross-referencing and integration of information. Essentially, investors are calling for improving elements of transparency and quality in financial reporting. We consider each of these suggested improvements next.

Investors' Top Priorities for Improving Financial Reporting: The Gap

Members indicated that the following financial reporting reforms are of greatest importance to them:

Greater Emphasis on Matters of Importance

A top priority for investors is greater emphasis on matters of importance in a particular accounting period, including an improved management discussion and analysis (MD&A) that explains the current period's results and expected future results. As Figure 1 shows, 85% of survey respondents indicated that improvements in this area are very important.

Figure 1. Investor Priorities vs. Standard Setter Focus

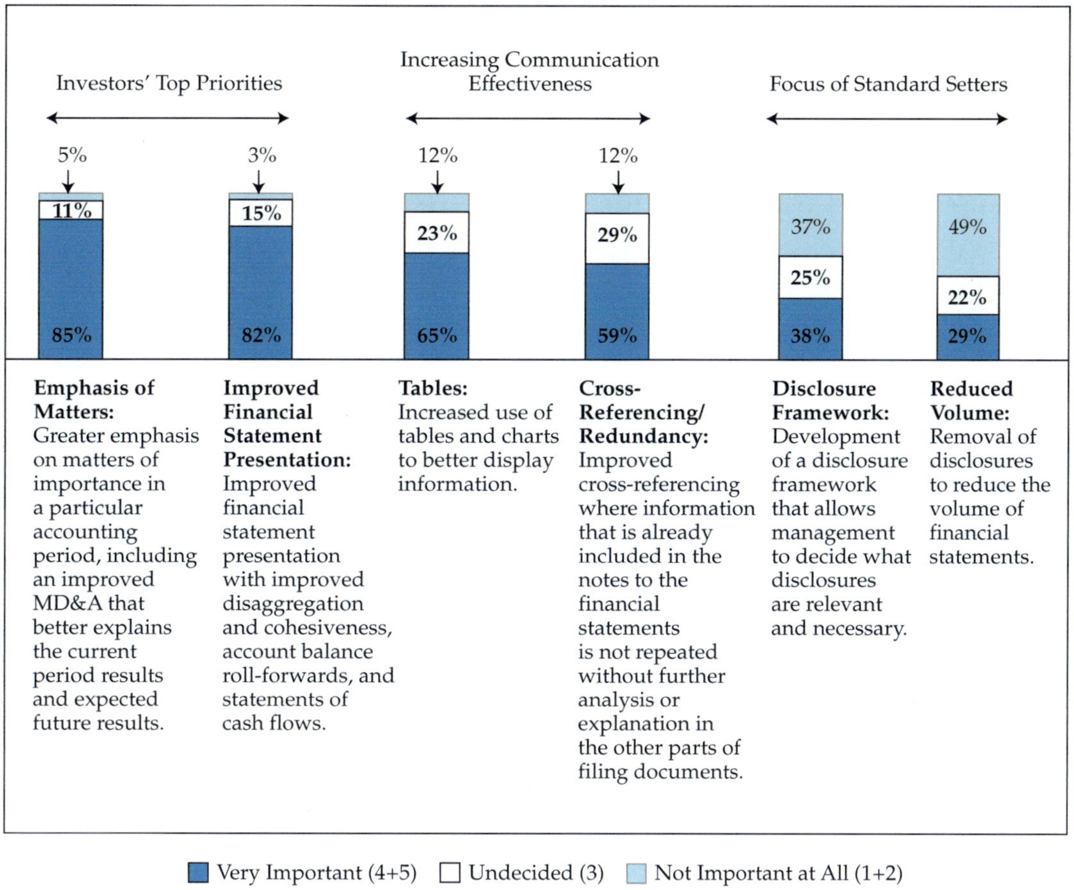

Notes: The question was, How important would each of the following potential financial reporting changes be to you in the use of financial statements? As for responses, $N = 303$.

Not all disclosures are important all the time. Within the entire collage of information needed to provide users with a sufficient understanding of the business, emphasis needs to be on disclosures of particular importance at a particular time in the economic environment. Additionally, highlighting the most important information during the current reporting period should not be seen as a substitute for providing a comprehensive story of the business. Furthermore, the analyst and investor community do not see these matters of emphasis as the only matters of importance or as substitutes for their own thorough analyses and rigorous investment decision making.

Investors should not be left to "connect the dots," as was the case, for example, in MF Global. Explicit articulation, summarization, and emphasis on matters of importance or significance should be included in the financial statements. Key messages should be obvious and clear, and investors should not be left to glean or decode them from compliant but uninformative disclosures.

Improved Financial Statement Presentation

Of the respondents, 82% considered improved financial statement presentation with improved disaggregation and cohesiveness, account balance roll-forwards, and statements of cash flows (Principles 9 and 10 of the *CBRM*) as very important.[16]

Importance of Financial Statement Presentation Relative to the Disclosure Framework Project

It has long been our view that before embarking on financial reporting disclosure reform, the IASB and FASB first need to determine what will be presented in the basic financial statements. Then, the standard setters can determine what disclosures best complement presentation.

Accordingly, in addition to asking respondents to our 2012 Disclosure Survey to prioritize their views on financial reporting and disclosure reforms, as reported in Figure 1, we asked members about their views on financial statement presentation and its importance relative to the disclosure framework project. As **Figure 2** shows, 85% of respondents believe that how information is displayed (presented) is an issue that should be addressed before a disclosure framework is developed.

Investors with whom we discussed the issue believe that the financial statement presentation project should not only be reinstated but should also be completed before an effective disclosure framework can be developed. Because presentation is the foundation of financial reporting, with disclosure being an explanation of the amounts presented in the financial statements, investors believe focusing on the disclosure framework without improving financial statement presentation is akin to building a house without establishing a proper foundation.

[16]These two *CBRM* principles are (1) Principle 9, Direct Method Cash Flow, which calls for the cash flow statement to provide information essential to the analysis of a company and to be prepared by use of the direct method only, and (2) Principle 10, Disaggregation, which calls for changes affecting each of the financial statements to be reported and explained on a disaggregated basis.

Figure 2. Financial Statement Presentation Priority over Disclosure Framework

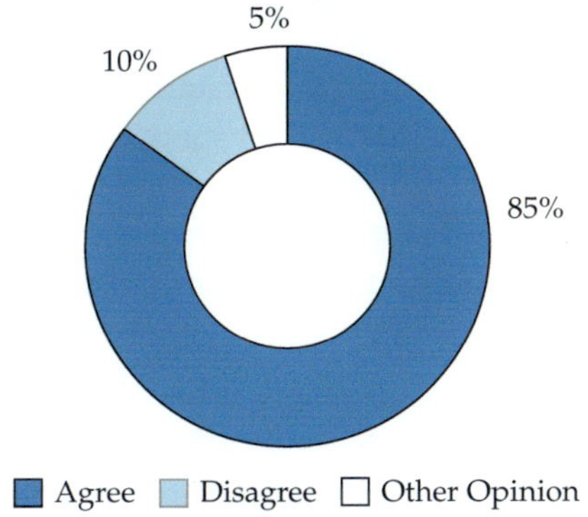

Notes: The question was, Do you agree or disagree that before developing a disclosure framework, as a first step, standard setters should simply reconsider how information is currently displayed in the financial statements? As for responses, *N* = 277.

Essential Elements of Improving Financial Statement Presentation

We do not think the financial statement presentation project previously undertaken has to be completed in the form in which it was originally devised. We believe that to substantially improve financial statement presentation and allow disclosures to be more transparent and effectively developed to explain the amounts presented in the basic financial statements, a simple focus on providing at least the following four elements is desirable:

- *disaggregation*—require sufficient disaggregation of main financial statements,
- *roll-forwards*—include roll-forwards of key balance sheet accounts,
- *cohesiveness*—implement a cohesiveness principle across financial statements such that investors are able to follow transactions through the various financial statements, and
- *direct cash flow statement*—require the use of the direct cash flow statement.

Previous Survey Results Echo This Message and Show Investors Prioritize Financial Statement Presentation over Convergence Projects Currently Under Way

Our 2010 Survey on Memorandum of Understanding Projects was meant to establish what our members viewed as key priorities with respect to IASB and FASB convergence efforts. As **Figure 3** shows, our members found the financial statement presentation project to be more important than the four convergence projects currently prioritized by the IASB and FASB and second only to the fair value standard, which has been completed.

The message is clear. Investors repeatedly stress the importance of improving financial statement presentation over nearly all other priorities.

Our Message to the IASB on Its Agenda Consultation

Therefore, CFA Institute stated in a comment letter to the IASB on its 2011 Agenda Consultation that the significant standard-setting development effort carried out in the past on financial statement presentation should be harnessed and the project should be reinstated as

Figure 3. **Financial Statement Presentation: High-Priority Project**

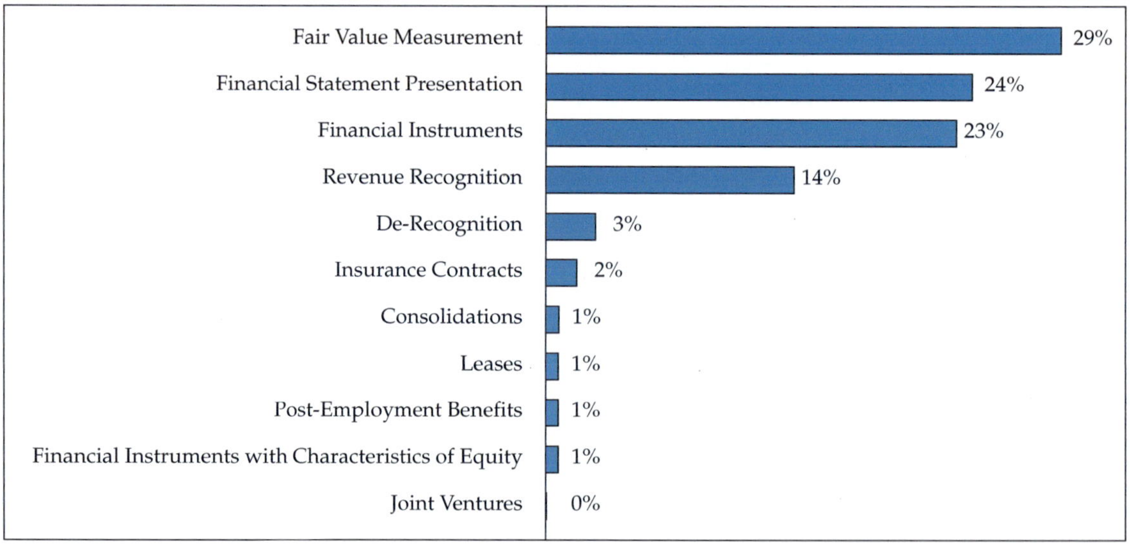

Note: As for responses, N = 489.

a priority of the IASB.[17] The importance of this project to investors has been established by considerable feedback from user representatives on innumerable occasions. The IASB's own User Summary from the 2011 Agenda Consultation showed that investors place financial statement presentation and other comprehensive income at the top of the list of what they believe the IASB priorities should be.[18] Unfortunately, the IASB final report on the 2011 Agenda Consultation makes no mention of the financial statement presentation project per se. The only discussion of presentation is in the context of the conceptual framework and the presentation of other comprehensive income:

> We see the presentation sections of the framework as being pivotal because the main financial statements (profit or loss, cash flows and financial position) are the windows into the activities of the reporting entity. Of particular importance will be how financial performance is presented, including consideration of the role of other comprehensive income (OCI) and recycling.[19]

Increasing Communication Effectiveness (Organization, Layout, and Style Changes): Common Ground

Our survey revealed that preparers and investors may find common ground in the pursuit of improving financial reporting and disclosure effectiveness in the following two areas:

Increased Use of Tables and Charts

A substantial majority of respondents (65%) indicated that the increased use of tables and charts would be very important to improving financial reporting. One survey respondent's comment puts it best:

---

[17]CFA Institute Comment Letter on IFRS Agenda Consultation (November 2011): http://www.cfainstitute.org/Comment%20Letters/20111130_3.pdf.

[18]User Feedback on 2011 Agenda Consultation (January 2012): http://www.ifrs.org/Documents/AC0112b05B.pdf.

[19]IFRS, "Feedback Statement: Agenda Consultation 2011," IFRS Foundation (December 2012): http://www.ifrs.org/Current-Projects/IASB-Projects/IASB-agenda-consultation/Documents/Feedback-Statement-Agenda-Consultation-Dec-2012.pdf.

> I love the simplicity of tables and charts when they present useful information. They're easy to read and understand. Narratives can sometimes be good, but when they become boilerplate or redundant, it's easy to just skip over it.

Improved Cross-Referencing/Eliminating Redundancies

The survey question found that 59% of respondents believe that financial reporting could be significantly enhanced by improved cross-referencing and elimination of redundancies. This finding is consistent with the results discussed in Section 4; a significant minority (33%) of respondents to the survey believe that the primary objective of the disclosure framework project should be to better integrate disclosure information in the various parts of the annual report. Overall, integrated presentation of related information enhances understanding of the relationship between items across financial statements.

These presentational changes could be attained by, for example, layering information, with summary information first and details later or standing information placed separately, perhaps as a schedule to the financial statements.[20] Such changes would address a common complaint about important information being buried among boilerplate, generic clutter, or standing information. Specific recommendations for reorganization that are consistent with what we hear from investors were included in a recent blog post titled "Improving Transparency in Note Disclosures: Can FASB Make the 'Hard' Decisions?"[21] The authors recommend the following changes:

- *Link financial statement line items to notes.* Each financial statement line item in both the balance sheet and income statement should be supported by note disclosure.
- *Number notes consistently with financial statement presentation.* The numbering sequence of the notes should be driven by the ordering of assets, liabilities, and stockholders' equity in a company's balance sheet, followed by the sequencing of specific income statement and cash flow line items.
- *Reconcile amounts presented in notes to financial statements.* Each balance sheet and income statement amount reported should exactly match the related note disclosure and any supporting schedule provided.

[20]Long-standing explanatory material should not be removed from the financial statements because it may still be relevant; it may be especially useful to a new investor in the company.
[21]Anthony H. Catanach, Jr., and J. Edward Ketz, aka Grumpy Old Accountants (August 2012).

- *Include accounting policies in the notes to which they relate.* Accounting policies for specific balance sheet and income statement components should be included together with the specific note disclosures.

These suggestions are just a few of possible improvements in how financial reporting is displayed that would make the information more digestible and effective in communicating a company's overall results. The FASB Invitation to Comment (FASB ITC) and the European Financial Reporting Advisory Group Discussion Paper (EFRAG DP) on the disclosure framework—both of which were issued in mid-2012—include suggestions on communication enhancements, which we support.

Investor-Focused Disclosure Reform Agenda

Figure 1 illustrates that investor priorities (emphasis on matters of importance and improved financial statement presentation) are very different from standard setter and policymaker priorities (disclosure framework and reduction of volume). Common ground exists, however, on the need to enhance the communication and presentational elements of financial reporting (tables, cross-referencing, and redundancy).

A PricewaterhouseCoopers 2011 report titled "Practical Guide to IFRS: Streamlining the Annual Report" arrived at similar findings, as evidenced by the following quotation:[22]

> We believe that the *transparency* and *connectivity* of the information is the *most important factor* in effective reporting.
>
> It is *not the volume of disclosure that matters* but its *quality and the way it is organized.* In the main, *users complain not about the length of the annual report* but about finding it hard to access the information they need. (p. 2)

Our findings suggest standard setters should refocus their efforts on enhancing quality and transparency in the areas that investors see of greatest importance to them—emphasis on matters of importance, financial statement presentation, and increased communication effectiveness.

[22]Available at www.pwc.com/gx/en/corporate-reporting/corporate-reporting-guidelines/streamlining-the-annual-report.jhtml.

In Section 8, we articulate our recommendations related to these findings. We also incorporate recommendations from our previous CFA Institute surveys. Those topical areas seen as needing greatest improvement in our 2003 and 2007 Corporate Disclosure Surveys proved to be the most problematic during the 2008 global financial crisis (see Appendix B), including off-balance-sheet items, cash flows, fair value, risk disclosures, derivatives, and hedging.

The development of a disclosure framework is not a top priority for investors, but it has been an area of focus for standard setters. Therefore, the next section discusses recent efforts made in this area and investor views on the specifics of the disclosure framework initiatives.

4. Disclosure Framework: Efforts and Objectives

Efforts are under way by the FASB and the EFRAG to create an overarching framework to make financial statement disclosures more effective and coordinated and less redundant.

Recent Disclosure Framework Efforts

The FASB added the disclosure framework project to its agenda in response to requests and recommendations from several constituents, including the SEC Advisory Committee on Improvements to Financial Reporting (CIFiR). The CIFiR was established by the SEC to study complexity and transparency in financial reporting. This committee issued a report just prior to the height of the financial crisis in August 2008 (the CIFiR Final Report), with 25 recommendations. Recommendations 2 and 3 of the report relate to the disclosure framework:[23]

> Recommendation #2: *The SEC and the FASB should work together to develop a disclosure framework to:*
>
> - Integrate existing SEC and FASB disclosure requirements into a cohesive whole to ensure meaningful communication and logical presentation of disclosures based on consistent objectives and principles. This would eliminate redundancies and provide a single source of disclosure guidance across all financial reporting standards.
> - Require disclosure of the principal assumptions, estimates, and sensitivity analyses that may impact a company's business, as well as a qualitative discussion of the key risks and uncertainties that could significantly change these in the financial statements, as well as events and uncertainties that are not recorded. (p. 8)

[23]CIFiR, "Final Report of the Advisory Committee on Improvements to Financial Reporting to the United States Securities and Exchange Commission," CIFiR (1 August 2008): www.sec.gov/about/offices/oca/acifr/acifr-finalreport.pdf.

> Recommendation #3: *The SEC and FASB should* also establish a process of coordination for the Commission and the FASB to regularly *assess the continued relevance of disclosure guidance in both bodies of literature*, particularly as new FASB standards are issued. *Existing guidance should be updated or removed, as appropriate.* (p. 9)

The stated objective of the FASB project is to develop a framework that will improve the effectiveness of financial statement disclosures, address concerns that some constituents have expressed about so-called disclosure overload, and guide the FASB in its development of disclosure requirements of individual standard-setting projects. This framework is expected to enable companies to communicate more effectively with investors, help eliminate redundancy, move away from what some assert has become a compliance exercise, and perhaps facilitate XBRL electronic tagging of information.

As an initial step, the IASB asked the Institute of Chartered Accountants of Scotland (ICAS) and the New Zealand Institute of Chartered Accountants (NZICA) to undertake a joint effort. The result is a report titled "Losing the Excess Baggage: Reducing Disclosures in Financial Statements to What's Important" (which we refer to as the ICAS/NZICA "Excess Baggage" report).[24] The terms of reference (p. 132 of the report) ask the ICAS and NZICA to review the level of disclosure requirements in IFRS and recommend deletions and changes to disclosure requirements—for annual financial statements of publicly accountable entities. The ICAS/NZICA "Excess Baggage" report, which did not appear to include any substantive investor input, suggests removal of numerous disclosure requirements from IFRS.

The IASB has added to its agenda a short-term initiative to explore opportunities to see how those applying IFRS can improve and simplify disclosures. The IASB conducted a survey on financial disclosure information and organized a Disclosure Forum to bring together securities regulators, auditors, investors, and preparers to discuss the current state of financial disclosures. Information received from this process will be used as input in the disclosure parts of the IASB's conceptual framework project.

Current Disclosure Framework Focus: Preparers

Much of the focus related to the disclosure framework project specifically, and disclosure reform broadly, has been guided by the views of the preparer community. Because most preparers are not familiar with the analytical and valuation concepts associated with performing

[24]"Losing the Excess Baggage: Reducing Disclosures in Financial Statements to What's Important," ICAS and NZICA (2011): http://www.nzica.com/reducingdisclosures.aspx.

financial analysis and making investment decisions, they do not have an understanding or appreciation of how financial statements are used by analysts or investors. Accordingly, the perspectives of investors appear underrepresented in this dialogue.

Recent reports that have been informing the dialogue on disclosures include those in **Exhibit 1**. The reports prepared by the Financial Reporting Council (FRC) include interviews with investors. As we note in the sections that follow, several of the investor observations noted in the FRC reports are consistent with what we hear from investors. We observe, however, that many of the conclusions appear weighted more toward preparer views.

Exhibit 1. Recent Reports on Disclosures

Issuing Organization	Report
U.K. Financial Reporting Council (FRC)	"Louder than Words: Principles and Actions for Making Corporate Reports Less Complex and More Relevant" (2009)
	"Cutting Clutter: Combating Clutter in Annual Reports" (2011)
Institute of Chartered Accountants of Scotland (ICAS) andNew Zealand Institute of Chartered Accountants (NZICA)	"Losing the Excess Baggage: Reducing Disclosures in Financial Statements to What's Important" (2011)
KPMG and Financial Executive Institute's (FEI's) Financial Executive Research Foundation (FERF)	"Disclosure Overload and Complexity: Hidden in Plain Sight" (2011)

The ICAS/NZICA "Excess Baggage" report makes no mention of investor input or investor views. The findings are not consistent with what we hear from investors. Moreover, the KPMG "Hidden in Plain Sight" report is based solely on a survey of preparers of financial statements. Accordingly, the findings are limited.[25] As the KPMG report notes:

> *If financial information users such as an investor community group had been surveyed, other valuable perspectives would have been obtained.* Since the data collection in this phase of this project did not solicit user input except through the consideration of academic literature and the consideration of the results of a single polling question posed at the winter 2011 Audit Committee Institute conferences, *this paper is limited in that regard.* (p. 3)

[25]KPMG, "Disclosure Overload and Complexity: Hidden in Plain Sight" (2011): www.kpmg.com/us/en/issuesandinsights/articlespublications/pages/disclosure-overload-complexity.aspx.

We appreciate the preparer voice in the debate regarding financial disclosures, but without substantial consideration of the views of the investor community, the relevance and validity of the findings in any such report are limited.

Focus of Recent Efforts: Quantity as an Objective

The principal view expressed in recent reports is that excessive disclosure is burdensome and can overwhelm users or cause them to miss relevant information. Such emphasis is evident through the titles of these publications. The disclosure framework has come to be seen by many preparers as a solution to the problem of financial reporting—that of lengthy disclosures.

The focus on volume can also be seen in the FASB ITC and the EFRAG DP material on a disclosure framework. Although both documents state that the objective of the disclosure framework is to improve the effectiveness of disclosures, the discussion quickly turns to reducing volume. Increasing effectiveness is largely seen to be equated with a reduction in quantity. The FASB ITC emphasizes this point:

> The disclosure framework described in this Invitation to Comment is based on the idea that excessive disclosure is burdensome to reporting entities and can overwhelm users or lead them to overlook important information. (p. 7)

The EFRAG DP makes the following point:

> It is suggested that a Disclosure Framework will play an important role in improving the quality of disclosures. The notion of quality is defined as improving relevance and logical organization of information and simplifying the preparation and use of disclosures. Although reducing the length of the notes to financial statements is not the primary intent, a sharper focus on relevance will likely result in reducing their volume, which is a legitimate expectation.[26]

This focus can also be seen in the November 2012 IASB press release announcing the intention to host a public Disclosure Forum "… to consider the challenging area of disclosure overload."

Although the FASB, IASB, and EFRAG indicate disclosure reform efforts are not about volume, much of the dialogue and communications are focused around this issue.

---

[26]"Towards a Disclosure Framework for the Notes," p. 17.

Some investor bodies, however, have expressed their concern over the expected outcome of the disclosure framework. An example is the Investors Technical Advisory Committee (ITAC), an advisory group to the FASB. The 13 December 2012 ITAC comment letter in response to the FASB ITC expresses concerns over the objective of the disclosure framework:[27]

> We offer a word of caution. Some of us are concerned that this project is seen by companies as an opportunity to remove an enormous amount of information from public disclosures at a coordinated time. Removal of public disclosures on a one-off basis from companies often has drawn the attention of investors and has sometimes moved stock prices; however, a standard that would allow for coordinated, mass disclosure reduction by a large universe of companies at the same time (the standard's effective date) provides a more socially acceptable opportunity for substantive disclosure removal. *We would be very concerned if this standard leads to a mass reduction of disclosure in which users do not have the appropriate opportunity to evaluate what is being eliminated and whether they believe it is appropriate that such disclosures be eliminated.* (p. 10)

Given the number of companies that have failed or suffered huge losses (discussed in Section 2) and the widely publicized audit failures since the financial crisis, it is unclear why the focus is not on whether the work of preparers and auditors on disclosures is of requisite quality rather than on eliminating disclosures.

CFA Institute Survey: Investor Views on Disclosure Framework Objective

The 2012 Disclosure Survey asked our members for their perspectives on what could be done to improve financial reporting disclosures and how they believed the disclosure framework could be integrated with current disclosures. Key findings related to the disclosure framework are articulated here.

[27]ITAC comment letter responding to FASB ITC (December 2012):10.

Retain Specific Disclosure Requirements

As seen in **Figure 4**, the overwhelming majority (85%) of respondents supported the retention of specific disclosure requirements by accounting standard. Within this significant majority, two possible subsets of improvements were identified:

- *Guide specific disclosures with an overall disclosure framework.* A majority of respondents said that the best way to improve financial reporting disclosure information would be to develop a disclosure framework to guide decision making but also provide specific disclosure requirements by accounting standard.
- *Emphasize matters of importance.* A significant minority of respondents wanted specific disclosure requirements with a requirement to emphasize matters of importance.

A very small portion of respondents want the disclosure framework to replace the specific disclosure requirements. An even smaller percentage of respondents said the best way to improve disclosure information would be to reduce the volume of disclosures.

Disclosure Framework: Complement Specific Disclosure Requirements

One of the most radical recommendations that has been made is to develop a disclosure framework that simply articulates the principal disclosure requirements and have it replace the specific disclosure requirements within the individual standards.

CFA Institute members strongly disagree with this suggestion. Consistent with the results in Figure 4, **Figure 5** illustrates that a majority of respondents believe that the disclosure framework should complement, not replace, the specific requirements contained within the individual standards. Investor quote(s) from the survey say it best:

> Specific disclosure requirements in the standards should be maintained to help ensure disclosure consistency across companies for key standards.

> The framework should be more generic and explain the objectives and reasons. The individual standards should identify the specific details that each jurisdiction's standard setters deem necessary to meet the overarching objectives contained in the disclosure framework.

Figure 4. Support for Disclosure Framework and Retention of Specific Requirements

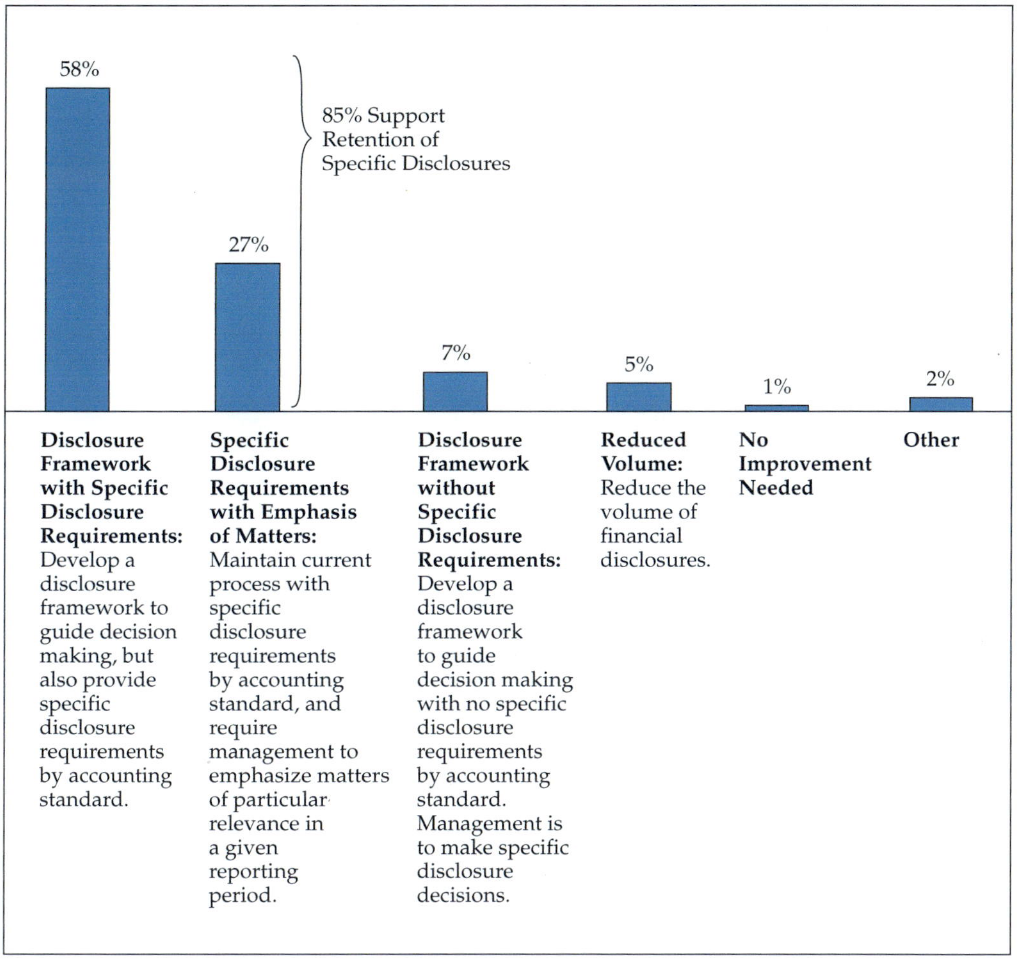

Notes: The question was, Which of the following best describes how, if at all, you would improve financial reporting disclosure information? As for responses, *N* = 323.

The disclosure framework should work in conjunction with the specific disclosure requirements. A general disclosure objective at the beginning of the disclosure requirements section in each standard is necessary to ensure that disclosures are focused. This will also ensure that the spirit of the disclosure requirements is achieved as specific disclosure requirements cannot account for every circumstance. Specific disclosure requirements are necessary to ensure investors receive detailed and disaggregated information presented in a comparable, understandable, and useful manner.

Figure 5. **Disclosure Framework: Complement, Not Replace, Specific Requirements**

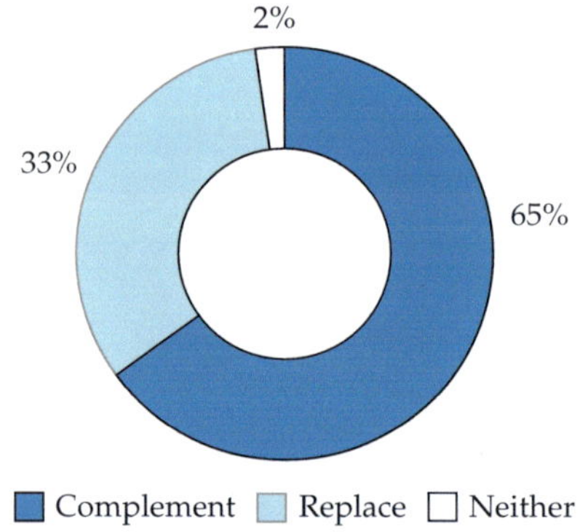

Notes: The question was, When developed, do you believe the disclosure framework should complement or replace the specific disclosures contained within the individual standards? As for responses, *N* = 220.

The results of another CFA Institute study, "User Perspectives on Financial Instrument Risk Disclosures under International Financial Reporting Standards: Volume 1," suggest that having a principles-based-only definition of disclosure is a significant contributing factor to uninformative disclosures.[28] (We will refer to this report as the CFA Institute "Risk Disclosures' report.") When guidelines are vague, a company can be in compliance with the rules without disclosing many useful details. The conclusions of the report are as follows:

> Overall… the reporting outcomes from IFRS 7 disclosure requirements illustrate that *a principles-based definition of disclosure is not the antidote to fears about boilerplate and uninformative disclosures. In fact, broad and vague definitions that are then described as principles are a significant contributory factor to uninformative disclosures.* The review of these financial risk disclosures shows that there remains a need for financial statement preparers to shift away from tick-box mere compliance with disclosure requirements. Preparers should *adopt a meaningful communication mindset* aiming to convey risk exposures and risk management policy effectiveness, as well as to foster a dialogue with investors. *Such a paradigm shift is necessary before a principles-based disclosure approach can result in substantially useful information.* (p. 2)

[28]Vincent T. Papa and Sandra J. Peters, "User Perspectives on Financial Instrument Risk Disclosures under International Financial Reporting Standards: Volume 1," CFA Institute (October 2011): http://www.cfainstitute.org/learning/products/publications/contributed/Pages/user_perspectives_on_financial_instrument_risk_disclosures_under_international_financial_reporting_standards__volume_1.aspx.

Primary Objective of Disclosure Framework Project

The results in **Figure 6** illustrate that members believe the primary objectives of the disclosure framework project should be as follows:

- *Increase effectiveness.* A majority of respondents indicated that the primary objective should be to increase the effectiveness of disclosures.
- *Better integrate disclosure information.* A significant minority believe that disclosures could be made more effective by better integrating disclosure information found in the various parts of the annual report.

Consistent with the results in Figure 4, Figure 6 reports that only 3% of respondents believe that the primary objective of the disclosure framework project should be to reduce the volume of disclosures whereas 96% indicate that more effective and integrated disclosures should be the focus. What is key is the *quality* of the information contained in

Figure 6. Primary Objective of Disclosure Framework: Increase Effectiveness

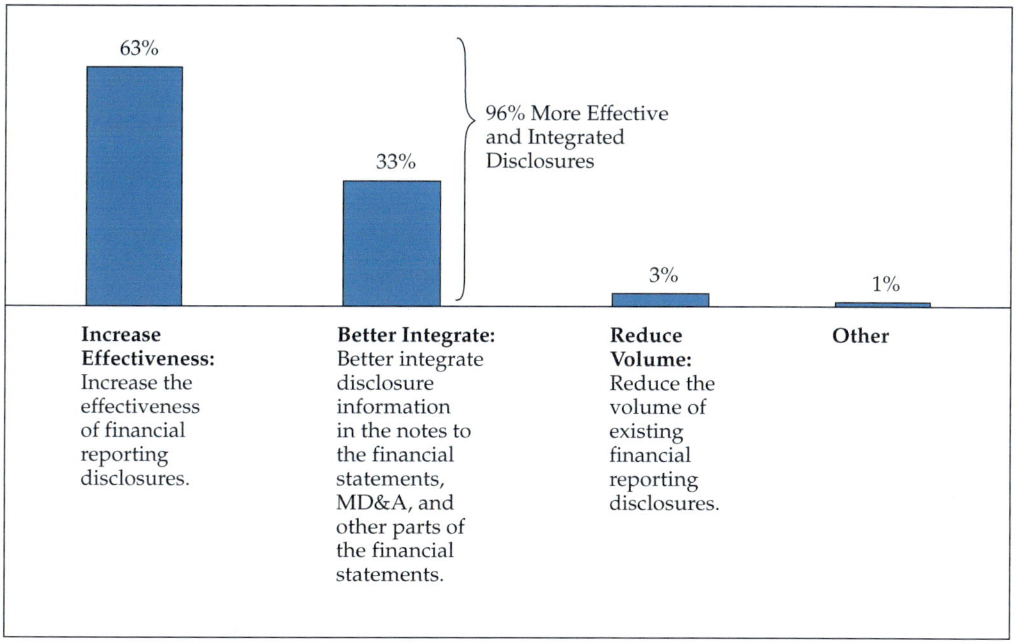

Notes: The question was, In your opinion, the primary objective of the disclosure framework project should be to. . . ? As for responses, *N* = 320.

the disclosures and how it conveys information about the specific reporting company to the reader of the financial statements. Overall, our members' view is that *optimal financial reporting does not necessarily equate with disclosure reduction but rather with disclosure effectiveness.*

CFA Institute's *CBRM*, described in the next section, sets forth principles for enhancing disclosure effectiveness.

Criteria for Development of Effective Disclosures

To ensure that disclosures provide effective and useful information and best serve investors' needs, the *CBRM* articulates eight disclosure criteria (on pp. 41–53) that should be applied when standard setters are developing disclosures and when disclosure requirements are being applied to companies' operations:

1. *Disclosure that complements recognition and measurement.* Disclosure is not a substitute for recognition and measurement, and recognition and measurement do not eliminate the need for disclosure.

2. *Concurrent development of recognition, measurement, and disclosure standards.* Standards for recognition and measurement of financial statement items and their related disclosures must be developed concurrently.

3. *Disclosure of judgment and choices.* Policy choices, assumptions, judgments, and methods must be fully and clearly disclosed.

4. *Disaggregation.* Disclosures should provide sufficient disaggregated information for investors to be able to fully understand and interpret the summary information in the financial statements.

5. *Disclosure of risks.* Investors require clear and complete disclosure of a company's risk exposures, its strategies for managing risks, and the effectiveness of those strategies.

6. *Disclosure of off-balance-sheet items.* Investors must have clear and complete disclosure of all off-balance-sheet assets, liabilities, and other financial arrangements and commitments.

7. *Disclosure of intangible assets.* Investors require clear and complete information about intangible assets held by a company.

8. *Disclosure of contingencies and commitments.* Investors require clear and complete information about a company's contingencies and commitments.

Results from previous surveys, as described in Appendix B, show support for these being key areas for improving disclosure effectiveness.

The Disclosure Framework Objective: Focusing on the Priorities of Those for Whom Financial Statements Are Prepared

The 2012 Disclosure Survey provides the much needed investor perspective on the disclosure framework objective and disclosure reform broadly. The results reveal that, although investors give other efforts a higher priority than the establishment of a disclosure framework, they do support a disclosure framework primarily designed to guide disclosures and emphasize matters of importance. Investors tell us that the primary focus of such a framework should be to increase the effectiveness of disclosures and better integrate information. Investors also support the retention of specific disclosures in the individual accounting standards to ensure that they receive the comprehensive, comparable, and disaggregated information needed for their financial analysis.

5. Investor Concern: Not Volume but Completeness of Information

Given the recent focus on the volume of disclosures as a key area in need of reform, CFA Institute members were asked specifically for their views on both the length and the content of current financial reporting disclosures.

Investor Views on Volume: Not a Significant Concern

A significant majority (80%) either do not have an issue with the length of current disclosures or think that, although current disclosures may be lengthy, they nonetheless contain necessary information. **Figure 7** displays the results.

- *More comprehensive story.* Half of the respondents indicated that volume per se is not the issue, but financial disclosures need to tell a more comprehensive story.
- *Emphasize matters of importance.* That current disclosures are lengthy but appropriate in volume was indicated by 14% of respondents. These investors indicated that disclosures do need to, however, emphasize matters of importance during a particular reporting period.[29]
- *Lengthy but necessary.* Another 14% of respondents indicated that current disclosures are lengthy but contain necessary information.
- *Currently satisfied.* One percent of respondents are satisfied with current financial reporting disclosures.

Only 18% of respondents indicated that disclosures are too long and believe the cause is redundant or unnecessary information. This result is in line with the results in Figures 4 and 6, where only 5% and 3% of respondents, respectively, indicated that disclosure information could be improved through a reduction in volume. One investor who took part in our survey said,

[29]This result is consistent with the results in Figure 4, where 27% of respondents indicate that they want specific disclosure requirements with a requirement that management emphasize matters of importance or particular relevance in a given reporting period.

Figure 7. 80% Say Volume Not a Significant Concern

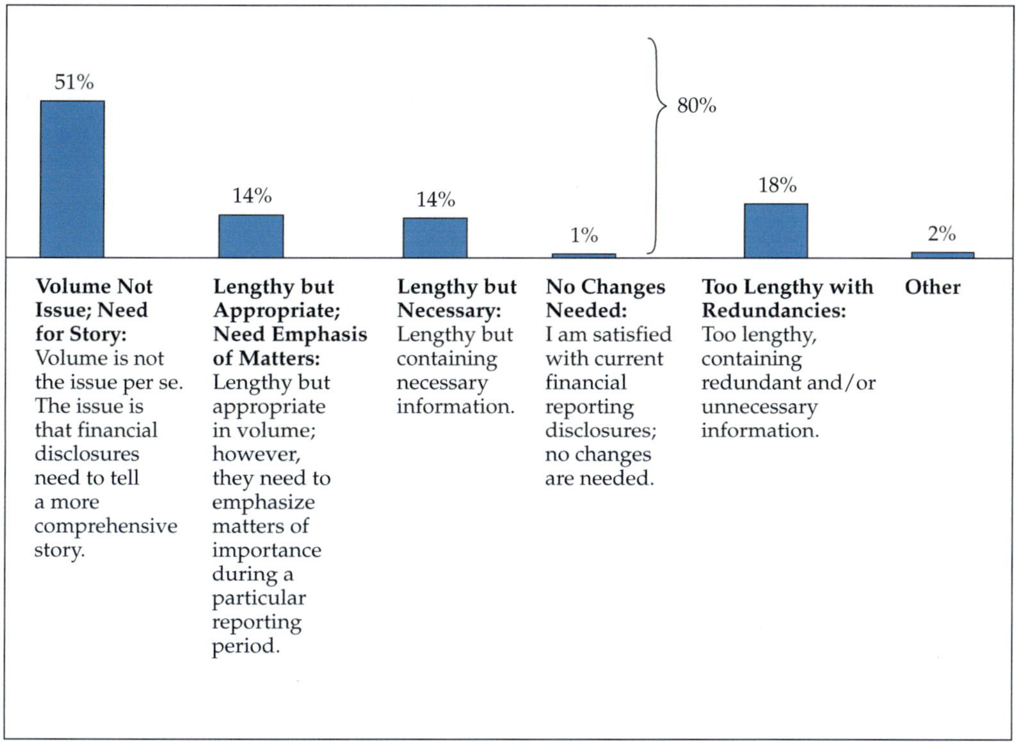

Notes: The question was, Which best describes your opinion regarding the length and content of current financial reporting disclosures? As for responses, $N = 325$.

> If you address the issues with respect to presentation, emphasis of matters and the display of information, volume will take care of itself. Financial statements are just the starting point for questions.

The FRC "Louder than Words" report acknowledges that investors do not necessarily believe that it is the length of disclosures that is the issue:[30]

> *Not everyone agrees that the length of reports is a problem.* Many large institutional users say they are happy for reports to contain as much information as possible, and they will decide what they want to use. (p. 18)

[30]FRC, "Louder than Words: Principles and Actions for Making Corporate Reports Less Complex and More Relevant," Financial Reporting Council (2009): http://frc.org.uk/getattachment/7d952925-74ea-4deb-b659-e9242b09f2fa/Louder-than-words.aspx.

What investors want is for financial disclosures to be more meaningful by conveying to the reader a comprehensive picture of the business and emphasizing key matters and significant transactions during a given reporting period. The ICAS/NZICA "Excess Baggage" report acknowledges this assertion:

> Disclosures should help "tell the story" about the performance, position and prospects of the entity. (p. 6)

Deleting Useful Disclosures Will Reduce Effectiveness

The ICAS/NZICA "Excess Baggage" report goes on to suggest removal of key IFRS disclosures is important to telling the complete story to investors. The report's suggestion, however, comes without indication of substantive investor participation. We believe that many of the suggested deletions will reduce effectiveness and create an excessive cost burden for investors.

Appendix B provides a summary of prior CFA Institute survey results on financial reporting disclosures. The results indicate the disclosures that investors rank high in importance but where they find the information not to be of high quality or overly aggregated or where they find there to be gaps in the information content. One reason for producing the *CBRM* was that CFA Institute found that several surveys of our members highlighted serious deficiencies in the financial reporting framework, problems that hampered their ability to analyze companies and make well-informed financial decisions.

We list here a few examples of the ICAS/NZICA "Excess Baggage" report's recommended deletions that we disagree with because they run counter to our long-standing positions as articulated in the *CBRM* and the results of member surveys referred to in Appendix B:

- *Reconciliations/roll-forwards*—Reduce the number of detailed reconciliations currently required. A summary of material changes should usually suffice. (See p. 7.)
- *Fair values*:
  - An entity shall disclose the fair value of classes of assets and liabilities in a way that permits it to be compared with its carrying amount. (See p. 39.)
  - For fair value measurements recognized in the statement of financial position, an entity shall disclose for each class of financial instrument (See pp. 40–41.):
    - The level in the fair value hierarchy.

- Significant transfers between levels.
- For level 3, a reconciliation of beginning and ending balances.
- For level 3, if changing one or more inputs to reasonable possible alternative assumptions, it would change the fair value significantly.

▲ *Contingencies*—Include details of contingent liabilities recognized in a business combination. (See pp. 23 and 25.)

Without substantial investor input on these deletions, there is a risk of deleting useful information.

Removal of Certain Disclosures: Investor Views

In an attempt to reduce the overall volume of financial disclosures, recent recommendations have proposed placing the onus on users to glean publicly available information—such as information on business risks, economic conditions, generally accepted accounting principles (GAAP), and other reporting requirements—from sources other than the financial statements.

In a similar vein, some have suggested that the summary of significant accounting policies be removed from the notes to financial statements and either be referenced or linked to a company website or possibly to relevant accounting standards.[31]

We asked our members for their views on these recommendations and what implications the recommendations could have for the boundaries, completeness, and relevance of financial statements.

As can be seen in **Figure 8**, 71% of respondents agree with the inclusion of the summary of significant accounting policies in the notes to financial statements. Footnote disclosure could be improved, however, by replacing boilerplate disclosures with ones that are specific to the company. Only 25% of respondents agree with the removal of accounting policy information.

[31]The ICAS/NZICA "Excess Baggage" report recommends introducing an "option for preparers not to repeat their summary of accounting policies in all financial statements but instead to give a reference to where those material accounting policies may be found e.g. an entity's website" (p. 7).

Figure 8. Investors Disagree with Exclusion of Accounting Policies

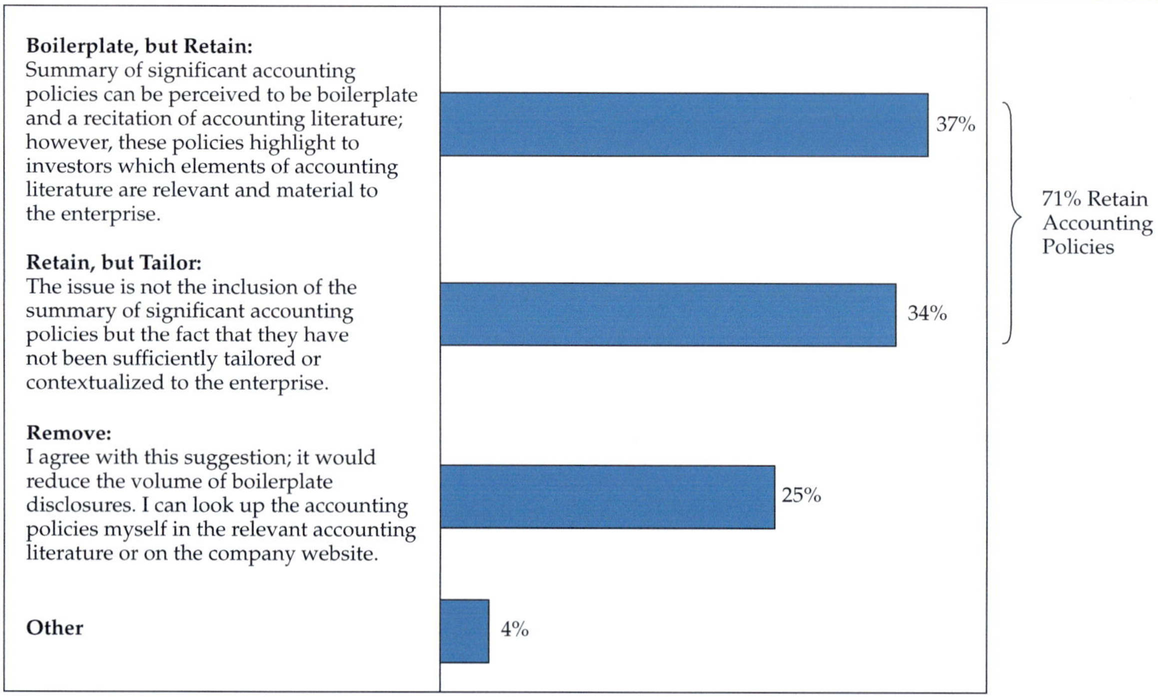

Notes: Participants were asked the following: The summary of significant accounting policies should be removed from the notes to financial statements and either be referenced or linked to a company website or possibly to relevant accounting standards. Which of the following best describes your view? As for responses, $N = 294$.

Included here are several representative quotes from respondents to our survey:

- Disclosures of significant accounting policies *MUST* [original emphasis] be made to enable users to know the bases of preparation of the financial statements, i.e. the methods for recognition and measurement of income, expenses, assets, liabilities, and equity. Users can then assess the suitability and other implications of the accounting policies. *Having to refer to outside financial reports for accounting policies is inconvenient and costly.*
- Financial reporting standards have choices of accounting methods. Hence accounting policies can differ across companies and for companies over time. Similarly critical risk factors and other matters requiring disclosures are specific to companies. *With this heterogeneity, having to refer to sources outside financial reports for disclosures on critical*

accounting policies and other important matters would add to the difficulty, inconvenience and cost of analysis. These negative effects would especially affect the poorer, less "sophisticated" and engaged users.

CFA Institute members have clearly told us that entities should be required to disclose a summary of significant accounting policies in the notes to the financial statements. Not all investors can be expected to be familiar with accounting literature and know where to find such information. Furthermore, we believe that the accounting policies should be tailored to the business so as to provide meaningful information to investors instead of a mere recitation of accounting literature.[32] Investors need to know management's rationale for making each accounting policy choice, the consistency of those choices, and the relative effects of the choices on the financial statements. Current accounting policy disclosure requirements are generally inadequate in this regard.

As noted in **Figure 9**, a significant majority of responding members disagree with the suggestion that footnotes to the financial statements not include information already readily available from public sources.

Figure 9. **Investors Disagree with Exclusion of Publicly Available Information**

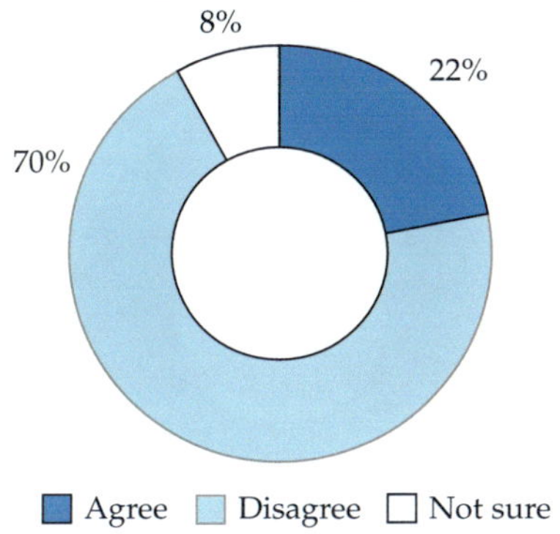

Notes: Participants were asked the following: The FASB suggests that footnotes to the financial statements not include information already readily available from public sources, information which may or may not be audited. Do you agree or disagree with the FASB's suggestion? As for responses, *N* = 251.

[32]For example, stating that fixed assets are depreciated over a range of 5–50 years does not provide useful information. Average life by class of fixed asset would enable investors to make comparisons with other companies with similar assets.

When asked about the ramifications of excluding certain information from the financial statements, 71% of respondents, as shown in **Figure 10**, answered that such exclusion would raise questions regarding the boundaries of financial statements and what represents a complete and relevant set of financial statements.

Survey respondents indicated several reasons for retaining information in the financial statements, including the following:[33]

- *need for comprehensiveness*—the belief that financial statements need to provide a comprehensive picture of the business,
- *need for completeness*—concerns over what will comprise a complete set of financial statements,
- *investor sophistication level*—the belief that less sophisticated investors may find it difficult to glean information from public sources,

Figure 10. Investor Concerns over Boundaries, Completeness, and Relevance of Financial Statements

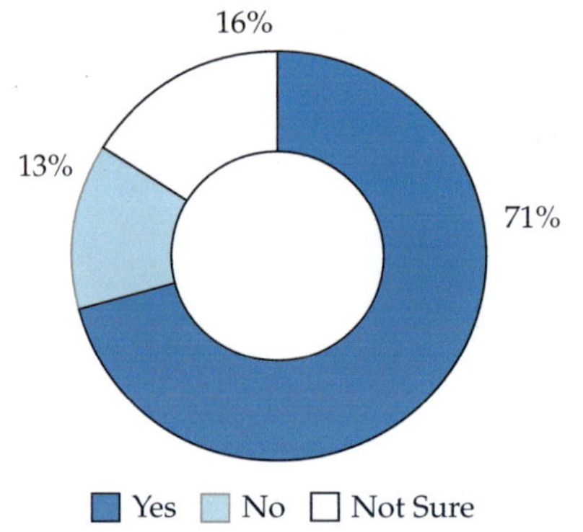

Notes: Participants were asked the following: If the FASB were to exclude certain information from the financial statements, do you believe this would raise questions regarding the boundaries of financial statements and what represents a complete and relevant set of financial information? As for responses, $N = 292$.

[33]The items in this list were developed from investor quotes in the survey responses.

- *concerns over accuracy*—concerns over the accuracy of public information,
- *need for audited information*—questions about whether the information will be audited or not,
- *dynamic information sources*—concerns over ever-changing information sources that may not pertain to the financial statements as of a particular date, and
- *costs to investors*—concerns that the costs of a multitude of investors looking up the information will far exceed the cost of one preparer collating the required data.

In the following paragraphs are several representative quotes from investors:

- Financial statements should provide a comprehensive look at an entity's financial condition. Directing investors to other sources to obtain a full picture of the entity's financial condition would prevent this goal.
- Although some investors are indeed sophisticated and can glean information from multiple sources, others are less so and shouldn't be made to make uneducated decisions or, worse, decide not to invest merely because access to information made the process too hard.
- The following questions will arise: What is the public source? How accurate is the public source? In what context does the information provided by the public source apply to the company in question?
- Information sources are dynamic. There needs to be a constant/stable source of information pertaining to the financial statements.

Sophisticated Investors Not Concerned with Volume

The 2012 Disclosure Survey results clearly demonstrate that investors are not concerned with the volume of disclosures.

The FASB and the Center for Audit Quality (CAQ) sponsored two forums on financial statement disclosure effectiveness in October 2012. Their findings are consistent with those of CFA Institute.

The FASB/CAQ Forum Observations Summary makes the following observation:

> Sophisticated analysts and users who are capable of analyzing high volumes of disclosure *did not express a significant interest in reducing the volume of disclosure.*

No Such Thing as Too Much *Useful* Information

We contend that investors cannot be overloaded with too much useful information. Additional useful information provides investors with greater transparency into their holdings, which, ultimately, reduces the cost of capital. This view is expressed in the *CBRM*:

> A protest that is frequently launched, either when additional disclosures are sought by investors or when standard setters propose to require them, is that investors are already overloaded with disclosures and cannot suffer the burden of any more. We would hasten to assure standard setters that *useful information is never overload.* Indeed, investors cannot properly conduct their analyses and make their financial investment decisions without it. (p. 40)

Information overload or useless information may come from various sources, such as redundant, boilerplate, and overly condensed information. We support eliminating redundant information that is repeated more than one time.[34]

Eliminating boilerplate and overly condensed information has been proposed by some—for example, in the case of significant accounting policy notes. This is not necessarily the right answer, however, because it does not automatically translate into greater efficiency, especially for investors. Instead, standard setters should be working to establish requirements that ensure that the information is not boilerplate in nature, is entity specific, and is sufficiently disaggregated to be meaningful.

[34]We support such elimination so long as the level of accuracy and audit assurance is not decreased because of the location of the information (e.g., including the information in the forepart to a registration statement rather than the audited financial statements). Investors need to be told the same thing only once, but its location for purposes of integration should not reduce its reliability. Many investors are not aware of the significantly different level of assurance associated with numbers presented outside the financial statements. We do not support movement of information out of the financial statements that has the secondary effect of reducing its quality and reliability.

The *CBRM* provides an example of the type of disclosure that is overly condensed and appears to provide quantitative or other detailed information but, in fact, provides little or nothing of substance:

> Our various classes of fixed assets are depreciated using a variety of methods, including straight line, sum-of-the-years' digits, and several declining balance methods, with estimated useful lives ranging from 5 to 40 years. (p. 40)

Such disclosures, often included in the accounting policies note, need to be disaggregated and made specific to the company. The objective should be to provide investors with useful information, communicated clearly and succinctly, in formats designed to convey the substance of the matter and what has changed and why.

Disclosures need to truly explain the economic substance of transactions or events. Accordingly, not only do we disagree with recent arguments for a reduction in disclosure volume, we go further and maintain that to provide investors with the transparency they require, disclosures should, if necessary, go beyond the requirements in the standards to provide investors with the requisite transparency. No list of disclosure requirements can comprehensively cover all transactions and events, and disclosure requirements generally lag new types of structures, instruments, and transactions.[35]

A 2011 ESMA consultation paper titled "Considerations of Materiality in Financial Reporting" echoes this view:

> An entity is also required to *provide additional disclosures when compliance with the specific requirements in IFRSs is insufficient to enable primary users to understand the impact of particular transactions*, other events and conditions on the entity's financial position and financial performance. (p. 13)

We will refer to this paper as the ESMA "consultation paper on materiality."

[35]The EFRAG DP states, "Disclosures in the notes are often provided on a checklist basis so although a particular disclosure may formally meet the requirement of a particular standard, it may not adequately explain the substance of a transaction or series of transactions or other events and conditions." (p. 60)

Volume: Not an Indicator of Completeness

Many preparers, pointing to the voluminous and ever-growing annual reports, posit that they must be burdensome for users to read. But these critics do not consider whether the information provided is complete. The volume of disclosures should not be assumed to be synonymous with providing complete and comprehensive information.[36]

Completeness: Only Marginally Addressed by Other Reports

The completeness of disclosures is only marginally addressed in other recent reports. They do not consider whether current disclosures, although voluminous, provide investors with a complete picture of the business. Is there information that is missing from the financial statements that would convey a comprehensive picture of the company's financial results to investors?

The FRC's "Louder than Words" report acknowledges that both *missing information and irrelevant details can obscure the overall message*:

> We have considered complexity in a broad sense, meaning anything that makes corporate reporting regulations or the reports themselves unnecessarily difficult to understand, implement or analyze. *This includes missing information or irrelevant detail that obscures the overall picture*. (p. 4)

Furthermore, it acknowledges that despite the increasing volume of disclosures, user needs are still not being met:

> Despite steadily increasing disclosure, *some really important user needs are still unmet—better cash flow statements and more detailed segmental reporting notes*, for example. (p. 19)

But the "Louder than Words" report does not go much further in exploring what is not being provided.

[36]As stated in Section 1, the same qualitative characteristics of financial reporting—understandability, completeness, relevance, and comparability—apply equally to financial statements and the related disclosures.

Disclosures: Hidden in Plain Sight or Missing?

Although many of the cited publications fail to consider the completeness of disclosures, KPMG's "Hidden in Plain Sight" report, even through its title, suggests that all the requisite information was in the financial reports prior to the financial crisis but investors simply missed the important disclosures because of the volume of disclosures.

"Hidden in Plain Sight" recommends (on p. 3) that the FASB and SEC undertake incremental procedures to ensure that an appropriate and adequate cost–benefit analysis supports all new disclosure requirements. It does not mention, however, the necessity of a review to identify what information the financial crisis demonstrated was missing from financial statements. This seems an obvious, but unasked and unanswered, question by many of those commenting on disclosure reform after the 2008 financial crisis.

Preparers and auditors indicate that there is already too much disclosure and that providing more will not be useful, but investors wonder what is being done, in light of the obvious evidence of disclosure shortcomings emanating from the 2008 financial crisis, to ensure that disclosures are complete and transparent. Investors posit that the benefit of greater and more transparent disclosures has already been empirically validated by the financial crisis. The benefit of enhanced disclosures surely outweighs the cost of compiling the disclosures.

In KPMG's most recent publication, "The Future of Corporate Reporting," the notion that disclosures were complete before the financial crisis is reiterated, as evidenced by the following comment:

> Admittedly, there were already warning signs to be found in corporate financial statements prior to 2008, *if people had looked hard enough*.[37]

Investors would surely disagree with this statement because it implies that they were provided with sufficient information; they simply did not look hard enough for it, or they missed it amid all the clutter. This line of thinking is troublesome to investors. It conveys a message that corporate managers and auditors were aware of the excessive risk taking (and communicated it to investors) but were unable to manage and mitigate the risks effectively. An alternative, and more plausible, hypothesis is that managers at these organizations, particularly the financial institutions, did not recognize or communicate to investors the possible implications and ramifications of certain of their business activities and risks under various scenarios. Lack of communication may have existed because (1) managers had not

[37]KPMG, "The Future of Corporate Reporting: Towards a Common Vision," KPMG (2013), p. 7: www.kpmg.com/global/en/issuesandinsights/articlespublications/pages/future-of-corporate-reporting.aspx.

fully identified the risks and uncertainties and/or (2) managers did not intend to provide a meaningful communication of the risks and uncertainties. Furthermore, our experience shows that when risks were recognized, measured, and disclosed in the financial statements, the managers focused more on the underlying risks (e.g., pensions).

We have referred to the aforementioned reports not to be critical of their contents per se but to highlight that they reflect a line of thinking that we see also in standard setter and policymaker reports framing their views with respect to disclosure reform. We find this line of thinking inconsistent with evidence that there has been a lack of disclosure resulting in decreased transparency and trust.

Overarching Focus of Disclosure Reform: Enhance Quality, Not Reduce Volume

Overall, we find the desire to remove disclosures to be inconsistent with investor views. Investors believe that the focus of the disclosure framework project specifically, and disclosure reform broadly, should be on addressing how to increase the quality, effectiveness, and completeness of financial statement disclosures. This is what our members have told us in response to the 2012 Disclosure Survey and to prior CFA Institute surveys on financial reporting disclosures (see Appendix B).

6. Complexity: A Disclosure Driver, Not a Result of Disclosures

As noted, the CIFiR was established by the SEC to make financial reporting information more useful and understandable to investors. The CIFiR had a charter to examine the U.S. financial reporting system in order to make recommendations to increase the usefulness of financial information and to reduce the complexity of the financial reporting system. The CIFiR report defined complexity in financial reporting and identified its causes. To the CIFiR, "complexity" refers primarily to the following difficulties:

- for *investors* to understand the economic substance of a transaction or event and the overall financial position and results of a company;
- for *preparers* to properly apply GAAP and communicate the economic substance of a transaction or event and the overall financial position and results of a company; and
- for *other constituents* to audit, analyze, and regulate a company's financial reporting.

The CIFiR report notes the negative effects of such complexity:

> Complexity can impede effective communication through financial reporting between a company and its stakeholders. It also creates inefficiencies in the marketplace (e.g. increased investor, preparer, audit, and regulatory costs) and sub-optimal allocation of capital. (p. 19)

Complex Businesses, Structures, and Transactions Drive Need for Disclosures

Increased complexity in businesses, structures, and transactions has driven the need for greater and more robust disclosure requirements. This need, in turn, has led to a necessary increase in the volume of disclosures.

The CIFiR report notes that the causes of complexity in financial reporting are many and varied and that at the top of the list of significant causes of complexity is the existence of complex activities:

The increasingly sophisticated nature of business transactions can be difficult to understand, particularly with respect to the growing scale and scope of companies with operations that cross international boundaries and financial reporting regimes. (p. 19)

Disclosure Volume Does Not Create Complexity

As enterprises grow larger and more complex, it is not surprising to see financial statements grow, correspondingly, in volume. The number of pages in a financial statement does not, however, necessarily equate with increased complexity. Nonetheless, many of the studies that have informed standard setters and policymakers have concluded that increased volume does add to complexity. The EFRAG DP makes the following observation,

> Some users prefer to have as much information as possible but *a number of studies [the FRC's 2009 "Louder than Words" report, the ICAS/NZICA 2011 "Excess Baggage" report, and the KPMG 2011 "Hidden in Plain Sight" report] have concluded that the volume of existing disclosures has added to the complexity of the financial statements and may confuse rather than inform users by obscuring relevant information*. In addition, such volume may result in an undue cost for preparers in managing and reporting extensive disclosures. (p. 17)

The ICAS/NZICA "Excess Baggage" report and the KPMG "Hidden in Plain Sight" report cited by EFRAG as informing on users' perspectives regarding volume adding to complexity and confusion for users actually included little—or in the case of the KPMG report, no—user input in their development. The FRC "Louder than Words" report, also cited by EFRAG, makes the following observation:

> *The diversity of views was a surprise.*
>
> The *preparers* we interviewed almost unanimously *believe that the process of compiling a corporate report is too complex*, and so are the reports themselves.
>
> In contrast, *users* discuss a number of shortcomings in annual reports but *do not consider them too complex overall.* They say they can dip in and out to find what they want. Those we interviewed do support the case for improvements to reporting, but seem to have *greater concerns about "relevance" than "complexity."* (p. 9)

It is concerning that standard setters and policymakers are looking to studies based on limited or no user input. Our experience tends to support the FRC "Louder than Words" report, where investors say they are more concerned with relevance than complexity or volume. High-quality disclosures can clearly communicate complex transactions and businesses. The issue is one of transparency of the transactions rather than their complexity or the number of pages.

Increase in Volume Is in Areas of Greatest Complexity

The KPMG "Hidden in Plain Sight" report contends that the volume of mandated disclosure requirements is one of the most significant contributors to complexity in financial reporting. It notes that "new disclosure requirements have been added over the last several years at an unprecedented pace" (p. 8) and lists recently adopted disclosure requirements in the following standards (also p. 8):

- disclosures about derivative instruments and hedging activities,
- accounting for certain convertible debt that may be settled in cash,
- disclosures about credit derivatives and certain guarantees,
- disclosures about postretirement benefit plan assets,
- transfers of financial assets and variable interest entities,
- fair value measurements and disclosures, and
- credit quality and allowance for credit losses.

The "Hidden in Plain Sight" report, using number of pages as a proxy for disclosure overload and complexity, finds that Form 10-K volume, on average, increased 16% over the six-year period reviewed; in contrast, the two banks included in the survey experienced increases of 53% and 110% over the same period.

Given the increase in the complexity of businesses and business environments over the past few years, the overall increase of 16% over the six-year period does not necessarily appear excessive. The report notes that in the areas pertaining to fair value, derivatives, and hedging, disclosures almost tripled over the six years, with a mean increase of 184%. These topical areas explain the substantial increase in disclosures for banking institutions.[38]

We maintain that it is the complexity of these very topical areas that has driven the need for new and robust disclosure requirements. That is, complexity has driven volume, not the reverse. The new requirements were necessary to ensure that managers provided adequate disclosure to explain these complex instruments, transactions, and measurements to the readers of the financial statements. For this reason, the most complex topical areas—fair value, derivatives, and hedging—have experienced the greatest increase in disclosure requirements.

Note, however, that the KPMG "Hidden in Plain Sight" report acknowledges that its study did not seek to identify what investors view as the key contributor to increased complexity:

> An important contributor to disclosure overload and complexity is increased complexity of transactions, investments, financial instruments, and relationships. This research did not attempt to identify the extent to which these considerations contributed to disclosure expansion. (p. 3)

We think a consideration of the root cause of complexity is important. Volume should not be used as a proxy for complexity.

Investor Views on Sources of Complexity

We concur with the CIFiR report, which defines financial reporting complexity from the perspective of investors, and those who analyze financial statements, as an inability to understand the economic substance of a transaction or event and the overall financial position of the company. Using this definition, the 2008 financial crisis exemplified complexity in financial reporting. Investors and other users of the financial statements were not able to understand or assess the financial position—specifically, risks—of many organizations and, most significantly, financial institutions. This definition of complexity also helps explain the increase in disclosures as business activities and transactions have become more complex.

[38]Romain Devai and Grégoire Naacke, "WFE/IOMA Derivatives Market Survey 2011," WFE/IOMA (May 2012). The report states that the number of exchange-traded derivative contracts doubled between 2006 and 2011.

Communication Regarding Complex Businesses and Transactions

As described in Section 4, the *CBRM* provides eight Disclosure Criteria that are meant to guide disclosures that facilitate this understanding and thereby reduce complexity. Investors understand that complexity in disclosures emanates from complex businesses and transactions; however, disclosures that do not provide sufficient transparency have a multiplier effect on increasing complexity. Escalating disclosure complexity because of increasingly global and complicated business activities and transactions is something investors will necessarily adapt to. Increasingly complex activities require more attention to, emphasis on, and reliance on the disclosure principles to ensure that the activities or transactions are clearly communicated and understood by investors.

An interesting illustration of this point is the disclosures made by MF Global in its financial statements regarding its "repo-to-maturity" transactions. When we contrast the descriptions in the MF Global financial statements to the descriptions, including diagrams, in the "Report of the Trustee's Investigation and Recommendations" to the bankruptcy court,[39] we note that the transactions had the capacity to be communicated, but the MF Global managers chose not to communicate them in a manner that facilitated an understanding of all the risks associated with the transactions. Because of this lack of clear communication, complexity was compounded.

Complexity Resulting from Accounting Standards

Investors also believe that complexity is increased by accounting standards that do not reflect the underlying economics of transactions or that fail to provide disclosures to allow investors to adjust to the economic measures the investors find most useful—that is, cash or fair value. Accounting standards that do not provide for appropriate recognition of transactions (e.g., off-balance-sheet vehicles, leases, executory contracts) require disclosures so users of financial statements can adjust to more economically relevant measurements. Similarly, standards that do not include appropriate measurement (e.g., amortized cost balances) require disclosures (e.g., fair value) to adjust to measurements that are more economically relevant to understanding an organization's financial position.

Poor financial statement presentation also adds complexity because it does not facilitate transparency or understanding of the financial position of the company or its transactions. For example, the inability to link income statement and cash flow captions (i.e., lack of cohesiveness) adds to the complexity of financial analysis for investors.

[39]"Report of the Trustee's Investigation and Recommendations, Regarding MF Global to the U.S. Bankruptcy Court Southern District of New York" (2012):66.

Furthermore, disclosures are sometimes meant to be a substitute for proper presentation (e.g., offsetting disclosures), which increases complexity. Overall, accounting standards may cause added complexity because they reflect a compilation of negotiated compromises that do not reflect economic reality and may or may not require the disclosures investors need to adjust to more relevant measurements.

Summary

Our experience with investors suggests three key sources of disclosure and financial reporting complexity:

1. complex businesses and transactions,
2. communications that do not meet the disclosure objectives outlined in the *CBRM*, and
3. accounting standards that do not clearly communicate the underlying economics of transactions or that use disclosures to substitute for appropriate recognition, measurement, or presentation.

7. Materiality: Where Is All the Immaterial Information?

We explore recent commentary on materiality, provide investor perspectives, and make recommendations.

Recent Commentary on Materiality

Recent publications have observed that annual reports are full of immaterial clutter that can obscure key messages or make important information hard to find. These publications encourage a continuing debate about what "materiality" means from a disclosure perspective and have made recommendations to enhance the use of materiality in financial reporting disclosures and to delete disclosures that do not contain material information.

New Terms: "Essential" Information

Certain standard setters and others have suggested that the disclosure framework should require only disclosures that are essential to investors. The co-chair of the joint working party that produced the ICAS/NZICA "Excess Baggage" report said,

> The current excess disclosure baggage carries the penalties of extra cost and poorer communication. We are recommending that preparers pack only the *essentials* into their reports. (p. 7)

The report recommends deletion of merely "encouraged" disclosures.

What is unclear is how "essential" is being defined. Does essential equate with material? We believe that what is essential is that all material information be disclosed in the financial statements. We also believe that care should be taken not to bandy about additional terms to define the threshold for the level of information to be provided in the disclosures when, already, we hear calls for clarification of the definition of "materiality" with respect to disclosure.

New Distinction: Material Item vs. Material Information

The ICAS/NZICA "Excess Baggage" report supports strict application of materiality and proposes the following:

> ... a refinement of how materiality is considered by distinguishing material items (being items in the statements of financial position, cash flows, comprehensive income and changes in equity) and material information which appears in additional notes to those statements: even though an item might be material, and therefore require separate disclosure on the face of the financial statements or in the notes, it does not follow that additional information about that item is necessarily material. (p. 2)

The report is unclear, however, about how to distinguish between a material item and the materiality of the information that pertains to that item. If an item is material enough to appear on the face of the financial statements, then it would seem essential that investors have the necessary information to understand the nature of the balance or amount presented on the face of the financial statements. Rarely would the financial statement caption be sufficiently descriptive to provide information on all the characteristics of the account balance.

New Applications: Exclusion vs. Inclusion

The FRC "Cutting Clutter" report goes further and argues that the application of materiality to disclosures should focus on exclusion of information, not inclusion. The report states,[40]

> It isn't just preparers' behavior that is creating barriers to cutting clutter. Those involved in setting standards, regulating, auditing and advising preparers about their preparation of annual reports are also contributing. Examples include the ICAEW's [Institute of Chartered Accountants in England and Wales's] guidance on materiality, which currently focuses on what to include rather than what could be taken out. (p. 14)

CFA Institute believes that, given the importance of disclosures as a complement to the basic financial statements, the focus should principally be on what information to include—not what information to exclude. A focus on exclusion could lead to the loss of valuable information for the investor community.

[40]FRC, "Cutting Clutter: Combating Clutter in Annual Reports," Financial Reporting Council (2011): http://www.frc.org.uk/Our-Work/Publications/FRC-Board/Cutting-Clutter-Combating-clutter-in-annual-report.aspx.

Continuing Concerns: SEC and Audit Comments

According to the KPMG "Hidden in Plain Sight" report, preparers identified concerns about materiality as contributing to increased disclosure volume. Preparers have articulated that concerns over SEC or auditor comments lead them to include immaterial information in the financial statements:

> Although both SEC rules and FASB standards make it clear that rules and standards need not be applied to immaterial items, we observed many companies providing these and other apparently immaterial disclosures. Based on the survey results as well as anecdotal conversations, companies are reluctant to omit disclosures other than those that are clearly immaterial, out of concern that an SEC comment or auditor comment will require the issuer to revise its reporting to include the immaterial item. (p. 21)

The report recommends that the SEC issue an interpretive release to address this concern. A possible solution identified in the report would be to include a single footnote that briefly identifies disclosures omitted based on their immateriality.

Another solution identified in the CIFiR report would be for the SEC and the PCAOB to adopt policy statements on how these regulators evaluate the reasonableness of judgments:

> We believe that adoption of these policy statements would not only provide more transparency into how the SEC and the PCAOB evaluate the reasonableness of a judgment, but also encourage preparers and auditors to follow a disciplined process in making judgments. (p. 7)

Books and Records Violations: Materiality vs. Reasonable Detail

SEC Staff Accounting Bulletin 99 (SAB 99), "Materiality," requires consideration of the books and records provisions under the Securities Exchange Act of 1934. Following these provisions, registrants have to keep books and records in reasonable detail to provide reasonable assurance to prudent officials. This threshold of "reasonable detail" under securities law is not necessarily the same as the materiality threshold under accounting standards. Indeed, in certain instances, "reasonable detail" could be a lower threshold. SAB 99 states,

> Even if misstatements are immaterial, registrants must comply with Sections 13(b)(2)–(7) of the Securities Exchange Act of 1934 (the "Exchange Act"). Under these provisions, each registrant with securities registered pursuant to

> Section 12 of the Exchange Act, or required to file reports pursuant to Section 15(d), must make and keep books, records, and accounts, which, in reasonable detail, accurately and fairly reflect the transactions and dispositions of assets of the registrant and must maintain internal accounting controls that are sufficient to provide reasonable assurances that, among other things, transactions are recorded as necessary to permit the preparation of financial statements in conformity with GAAP. In this context, determinations of what constitutes "reasonable assurance" and "reasonable detail" are based not on a "materiality" analysis but on the level of detail and degree of assurance that would satisfy prudent officials in the conduct of their own affairs. Accordingly, failure to record accurately immaterial items, in some instances, may result in violations of the securities laws.

Some contend that complying with this books and records provision of the Exchange Act and meeting the threshold of reasonable detail have resulted in immaterial information being included in financial statements. Before concluding that this provision is, in fact, a cause of the inclusion of immaterial disclosures, investors want to know whether preparers and auditors can clearly point to immaterial disclosures that have been included in financial statements merely to comply with the books and records provision. Investors have not seen a direct link between these provisions and the inclusion of immaterial disclosures in financial statements. Furthermore, investors question why greater disaggregation (detail) is not provided in financial statements if this requirement drives disclosures.

Materiality: A New Concept?

The application of materiality to disclosure requirements is not a new idea. Materiality has long been applied to financial disclosures by preparers and auditors alike. What appears to be changing in the current debate over the application of materiality to disclosures is the rather strict application recommended in recent reports.

In the materiality spectrum, certain items are clearly material and others are clearly immaterial. In the large grey area in between, however, significant judgment is needed when determining necessary disclosures. And information in this grey area that is useful for investment decision making should not be omitted from the footnotes. Without such decision-useful information, investors are ill-equiped when they make their resource allocation decisions. What investors have not seen—even in the post–Sarbanes–Oxley Act environment with its disclosure audit differences—is a substantial increase in disclosures of immaterial information. Linkage of this assertion to the inclusion of immaterial information needs to be demonstrated.

Perception vs. Reality: Research Needed to Demonstrate Increase in Immaterial Disclosures

In short, many generalized claims have been made that immaterial disclosures are being included in financial statements and that information needs to be curtailed to only what is essential. We believe, however, that more specific research is needed to find examples of inclusion of immaterial information before the conclusion can be drawn that extensive amounts of immaterial information are indeed being included in financial statements. For example, a review of the financial statements of the Dow Jones Industrial Average 30 companies could be performed to identify whether, or the extent to which, any immaterial disclosures have been made and, if so, why. Furthermore, investors and preparers for these entities could be interviewed and results developed based on both empirical and anecdotal evidence.

Investor View: No Obvious Inclusion of Immaterial Information

We surveyed members to gain their views regarding the impact of the enhanced use of materiality in financial reporting disclosures. The results displayed in **Figure 11** indicate the following:

- The majority (51%) of respondents believe it is difficult to discern what the impact will be because the application of materiality is a matter of judgment. If there was an obvious inclusion of immaterial information, investors would not find it difficult to discern whether enhanced use of materiality and deletion of disclosures would be significant.
- Another 25% of respondents indicated that the impact will not be significant.
- Only 20% indicated that the enhanced use of materiality will result in a significant reduction in information disclosed.

In summary, 76% of respondents do not currently observe the inclusion of obviously immaterial information in financial statements.

Figure 11. Investors Surveyed See No Obvious Inclusion of Immaterial Information

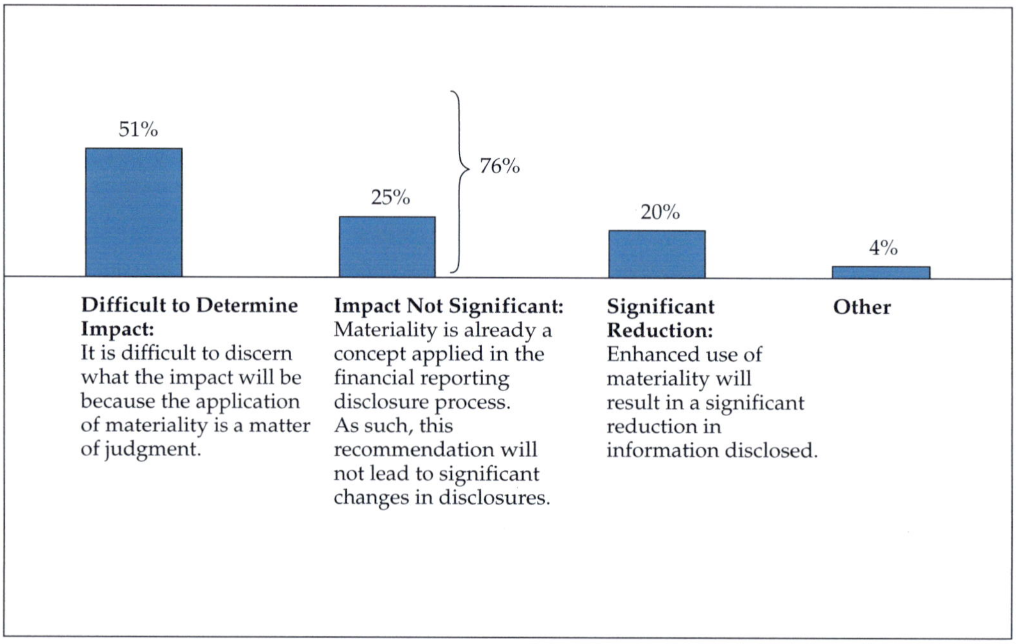

Notes: Participants were asked the following: Which of the following statements most accurately describes your view regarding enhanced use of materiality in financial reporting disclosures as well as the deletion of disclosures that do not contain material information? As for responses, *N* = 301.

Need for Investor Perspective in Materiality Determination

We underscore that the perspective of an investor must be central to the definition of materiality. We have long argued that materiality assessments for the level of information to be provided in the financial statements and disclosures should use the standard of whether the item or information disclosed would make a difference to the decision making of an informed investor. Investors' information requirements should determine the materiality threshold as articulated in Principle 6, Investor Materiality Threshold, of the *CBRM*.

The CIFiR report affirms this position in stating that materiality should be based on the "perspective of a reasonable investor" (p. 12). This view is echoed in Aqel:[41]

[41]Saher Aqel, "Auditors' Assessments of Materiality between Professional Judgment and Subjectivity," *Acta Universitatis Danubius Oeconimica*, vol. 7, no. 4 (2011):72–88.

> The concept of materiality is directly linked to the decision-making requirements of financial statement users. Materiality has been defined by the FASB in Statement of Accounting Concepts No. 2, Qualitative Characteristics of Accounting Information as... "The omission or misstatement of an item is material in a financial report, if, in light of surrounding circumstances, the magnitude of the item is such that it is probable that the judgment of a reasonable person relying upon the report would have been changed or influenced by the inclusion or correction of an item." (p. 73)

The ESMA consultation paper on materiality addresses what is needed in the assessment of materiality as follows:

> An assessment of materiality requires an understanding of the characteristics of the users of the financial statements of an entity, the attributes of the information required by those users, the purpose of the information being disclosed as well as other matters outlined in this Paper. (p. 7)

We also note that SAB 99 refers to investors and their assessments of materiality in reaching conclusions regarding materiality. We have found, however, that preparers and auditors have little training in investment analysis and decision making or interaction with investors. Thus, they may find evaluating materiality with reference to how investors might perceive materiality to be challenging.

Assessing Materiality: Expectations and Knowledge Gaps

Aqel (2011) identifies three problems in arriving at a materiality definition:

1. *All stakeholders make materiality decisions.* Materiality decisions are made by preparers, auditors, and users. These heterogeneous groups are likely to have dissimilar views concerning materiality. Aqel states,

    > Some studies have observed investors' materiality threshold based on their reactions to new earnings announcements. Cho et al., 2003, for example, investigated empirically investors' perceptions of materiality in the context of several materiality criteria that include percentage of pretax earnings, percentage of sales, and percentage of total assets by observing stock price

> reactions when unexpected information is revealed to stock market participants. The study pointed out that users demonstrate lower materiality thresholds than auditors.[42] This indicates the existence of [an] expectation gap regarding materiality. (p. 84)

One of the main conclusions drawn from the responses to the ESMA consultation paper on materiality is that the majority of all respondents believe that the concept of materiality is generally well understood but they see diversity in application. Diversity in application was attributed to management judgment, separate perspectives of different stakeholder groups, and general difficulties in applying the concept to certain issues.

2. *Limited information on how preparers and auditors make materiality judgments.* Limited knowledge is available about how materiality judgments are made by preparers and auditors and how they affect users' decision making.

3. *Limited understanding by preparers and auditors about the use of financial statements.* Very little is known about the ways financial statements are used by users in making their credit and investment decisions:

> Little information is known on how materiality judgments made by preparers and auditors will affect the users' decision making because limited knowledge is available on how financial statements are utilized by users in investment and credit decision making.[43]

Aqel explains his findings as follows:

> The FASB definition of materiality explicitly addresses decision usefulness of the financial statements users. However, in practice users are not involved in the concept at all. Users don't have enough knowledge about auditors' responsibilities. Furthermore the auditor's report does not include detailed information related to materiality. (p. 84)

To address these gaps in expectations and knowledge, education is needed on how investors use financial statements and how investors are affected by materiality judgments made by auditors and preparers.

---

[42]Aqel is referring to S.Y. Cho, S.N. Hagerman, and E.R. Patterson, "Measuring Stockholders Materiality," *Accounting Horizons*, vol. 17 (2003).

[43]G.L. Holstrum and W. Messier, "A Review and Integration of Empirical Research on Materiality," *Auditing: Journal of Practice & Theory*, vol. 2 (Fall 1982):48.

Furthermore, the CIFiR report recommends that the FASB or the SEC, as appropriate, conduct education sessions internally and make outreach efforts to financial statement preparers and auditors to raise awareness of materiality issues and to promote consistent application of the concept of materiality.[44]

Need for Communication: Disclosure of Materiality Judgments and Thresholds

Given the lack of consensus on materiality thresholds among auditors, preparers, and users, many users believe disclosures should be made in the financial statements regarding (1) the materiality judgments exercised by management and (2) the materiality thresholds applied by auditors in the conduct of their work in the auditor's report. Such disclosures would provide transparency and enable users to more easily assess the information presented in the financial statements. This practice would also resolve the knowledge and expectations gaps.

In March 2010, CFA Institute asked a group of members with an expressed interest in financial reporting issues their views on the disclosure of auditor materiality thresholds. As reflected in the survey report, "Independent Auditor's Report Survey Results," 82% of respondents agreed that the method by which the auditor determines/assesses materiality should be disclosed. **Figure 12** shows this finding.

Representative respondent quotes include the following:

- This will help the user understand what level of tolerable error to allow for analysis of the income statement and balance sheet. Importantly it should also be disclosed whether one materiality level has been applied across the income statement and balance sheet or whether there are differences.

- I would consider the materiality definition one of the most important matters, esp. in light of cases like HealthSouth.

- This is a key issue. GAAP calls on management to determine materiality. The auditors then provide judgment about management's determination. Managements need to make materiality hurdles clear and investors need to know what the auditor thinks.

[44]See the CIFiR report, p. 12.

Figure 12. Disclosure of Auditor Assessment of Materiality

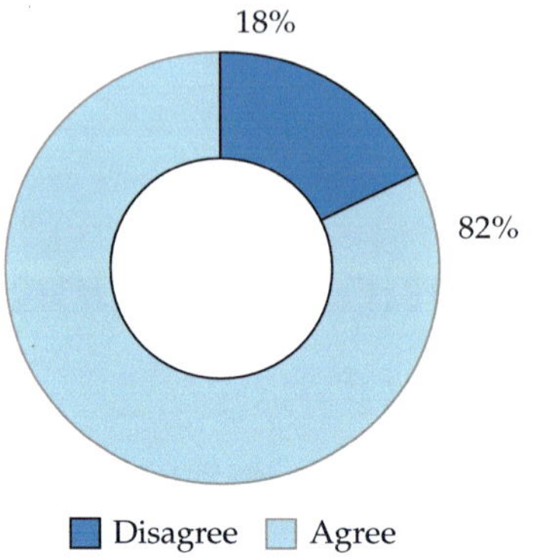

Notes: Participants were asked the following: Do you agree or disagree that the method by which the auditor determines/assesses materiality should be disclosed? As for responses, *N* = 144.

The ESMA consultation paper on materiality proposes an accounting policy note disclosing materiality judgments exercised by preparers:

> An entity shall disclose, in the summary of significant accounting policies or other notes, the judgments, apart from those involving estimations, that management has made in the process of applying the entity's accounting policies and that have the most significant effect on the amounts recognized in the financial statements. In this context a view could be taken that preparers of financial reports should carefully consider making disclosures regarding materiality judgments exercised in preparing financial reports with a view to providing the primary users with information that is relevant to the primary users' understanding of those financial reports. (p. 11)

The summary of responses to the ESMA consultation paper on materiality states that, although the inclusion of such information by other parties has little support, "a number of user representatives did see merit in the provision of such [accounting policy disclosure] information, either in the notes to the financial statements or as part of the report to the audit committee" (p. 4).

Concluding Thoughts on Materiality

As we consider the materiality issue in the aggregate, we can see that a perception has emerged among preparers and auditors that financial statements are filled with immaterial information. This perception has been communicated to standard setters through the reports cited in this document. The investors we surveyed, however, do not find an obvious overabundance of immaterial information. Issues relating to boilerplate information or lack of entity-specific information are of greater concern to investors.

This disconnect in materiality assessments likely stems from a lack of communication regarding the materiality measures and thresholds made by management and auditors. The knowledge and expectations gaps are obvious and natural by-products of the lack of communication. Without greater communication of materiality measures and thresholds, the inability of users to provide feedback regarding materiality and its impact on their decision making will persist.

8. Recommendations: Enhancing Financial Reporting and Disclosure Effectiveness

Throughout this document, we have stressed the importance of considering investors' views on financial reporting and disclosure recommendations in the context of factors they perceive as affecting the current financial reporting environment. Investors perceive financial reporting information as lacking transparency (see Section 2). Insufficient transparency creates distrust in the markets and a lack of investment in the broader economy. Investors tell us that the most effective way to enhance transparency would be for standard setters to prioritize certain financial reporting and disclosure improvements ahead of the establishment of a disclosure framework. Accordingly, we provide recommendations in the following areas in order of importance to investors:

- financial statement presentation,
- communication and presentational enhancements, and
- disclosures perceived by investors to be most in need of improvement.

All of the recommendations would eventually form part of a disclosure framework. Moreover, we have included other matters for consideration in the development of a disclosure framework.

Exhibit 2 provides a summary of the context and recommendations.

Financial Statement Presentation

As noted in Figure 2, our 2012 Disclosure Survey found that investors believe improved financial statement presentation is a key element to improving financial reporting broadly and disclosures specifically. This finding is consistent with previous CFA Institute surveys, all of which reflect investors' view that poor financial statement presentation limits transparency in financial reporting. *Disclosures are less effective when they exist to complement financial statements that are not an effective foundation to portray financial results or when disclosures are*

Exhibit 2. Recommendations Based on Factors Affecting Investor Views on Current Financial Reporting and Disclosure Environment

A. Factors

Financial Crisis/Great Recession:
Lack of Transparency → Lack of Investor Trust → Lack of Investment

Technology:
The Irreversible Trend toward Greater Connectivity and Data in Financial Reporting

Existing Accounting Model:
Providing Decision-Useful Information in the New Economy?

Measurement:
Resolving Measurement and the Disclosures That Make Measurements Meaningful

B. Recommendations

Financial Statement Presentation	Communication and Presentational Enhancements	Most Troublesome Disclosures	Considerations to Incorporate in Decisions to Improve Disclosures	Considerations Specific to the Development of a Disclosure Framework
1. Disaggregation	5. Integration	11. Estimates, judgments, and choices	18. Materiality	22. Focus on equity investors
2. Direct method cash flow statement	6. Entity-specific information	12. Risks	19. Technology	23. Include disclosure objectives
3. Cohesiveness	7. Emphasizing matters of importance	13. Off-balance-sheet items	20. Costs and benefits	24. Maintain specific disclosure standards
4. Roll-forwards of key balance sheet accounts	8. Organizing and layering information	14. Commitments and contingencies	21. Behavioral elements	25. Disclosures should be a focus, not afterthought, in development of standards
	9. Simple language	15. Intangible assets		26. Comprehensive information source
	10. Tables and charts	16. Going concern issues		27. Applicability (entities and reporting periods)
		17. Go beyond requirements if necessary		

meant to compensate or substitute for poor financial statement presentation. In many instances, disclosures have been required by standard setters *in place of* the appropriate presentation (e.g., offsetting requirements) and recognition and measurement (e.g., in the case of leases).

Overall, the message from investors is that improving disclosures without enhancing their *foundation*—the basic financial statements—will not substantially enhance financial reporting. To this end, our first four recommendations correspond to the four essential elements of improving financial statement presentation described in Section 3.

1. Disaggregation

Information in the basic financial statements is too highly aggregated. Greater disaggregation should exist so that investors can connect disclosures to the basic financial statements. Disaggregation is also important to investors because it enables them to understand the nature of underlying balances and to make better comparisons between and among companies and because it enhances the predictive capacity of the information presented.

2. Direct Method Cash Flow Statement

Companies should be required to prepare their statement of cash flows under the direct method. The direct method cash flow statement provides investors with the composition of cash flows, which investors can then correlate with earnings presented in the income statement. Cash flows and fair values, not accounting measurements, are important in valuing businesses. Therefore, including direct method cash flow statements will enhance substantially the usefulness of financial reporting. Including a direct method cash flow statement will also substantially reduce the use of—or, at a minimum, enhance the reliability of—non-GAAP measures, such as earnings before interest, taxes, depreciation, and amortization. In general, this method of cash flow preparation better equips investors with the information necessary to appraise a company's liquidity, assess its earnings quality, and make more realistic cash flow forecasts.

3. Cohesiveness

Improved cohesiveness of balances within and among the basic financial statements would improve the usefulness of financial statements by allowing investors to see the flow of transactions across the balance sheet, income statement, and statement of cash flows. Increased cohesiveness is likely to lead to the need for fewer disclosures because the necessary transparency and underlying relationships between balances that produce the financial results will be more obvious to investors.

4. Roll-Forwards of Key Balance Sheet Accounts

We call for an increased use of roll-forwards of key balance sheet accounts because they are an efficient way of transparently displaying both operating and nonoperating changes as well as cash and noncash effects on balance sheet accounts. They also help increase cohesiveness because they demonstrate the links between the balance sheet, income statement, and statement of cash flows.

Also important to investors is a project to define "other comprehensive income" and when it should be used.

Communication and Presentational Enhancements

This second category of recommendations relates to enhancements in communication style and presentation that could improve the way information is transmitted to investors and investors' understanding of financial reporting information. In the context of the findings of the 2012 Disclosure Survey as shown in Figure 1, the recommendations presented here relate to emphasizing matters of importance, increasing the use of tables and charts, and reducing redundancy by adding cross-references.

5. Integration

Between Financial Statements and the MD&A/Management Commentary

Disclosure reform should, where possible, better integrate disclosure information in the notes to the financial statements, MD&A or management commentary, and other parts of the financial statements. Where possible, cross-referencing of information should be used so as to avoid unnecessary repetition. We support elimination of duplication as long as the level of accuracy and audit assurance are not decreased because of the location of the information (e.g., including the information in the front of a registration statement instead of in the audited financial statements). Investors need to be told the same thing only once, but its location for the purpose of integration should not reduce its reliability. Many investors are not aware of the significantly different level of assurance associated with amounts presented outside the financial statements.

Within Financial Statements

We also see an opportunity to better integrate information within the footnotes to the financial statements to make disclosures more meaningful. For example, reporting that integrates the related financial statement captions, accounting policy footnotes, assumption disclosures, sensitivity analyses, roll-forwards, and detailed explanatory disclosure requirements, which collectively communicate a story related to the financial statement captions, would be helpful to investors.

6. Entity-Specific Information

Disclosure reform should promote financial reporting that is tailored to a company, that is entity specific. Accounting policies provide the best example of how financial reporting is not written to be entity specific; sometimes, the policies are a mere recitation of accounting literature. Such boilerplate information is not meaningful to investors. Furthermore, not all accounting policies are important all the time. The material needs to emphasize which accounting policies are of particular importance at a particular time in light of the economic environment. Accounting policies should also be linked to balances in the financial statements. The integration we suggest would provide better context and meaning to disclosures and point out which accounting policies may be especially important at a particular time.

7. Emphasizing Matters of Importance

Disclosure reform should promote the presentation of information in a manner that highlights matters of importance during a particular reporting period. Explanations should be given of current-period results, unusual and infrequent events or transactions, and expected future cash flows. Not all disclosures are important all the time. Within the entire collage of information needed to provide users with sufficient understanding of the business, the emphasis should be on disclosures that may be of particular importance. Highlighting the most important information during the current reporting period should not be seen, however, as a substitute for providing a comprehensive story of the business.

Investors should not be left to connect the dots in the financial statements. Matters of importance or significance should be explicit, articulated, summarized, and emphasized. Key messages should be obvious and clear. Investors should not be left to glean or decode them from compliant yet uninformative disclosures.

8. Organizing and Layering Information

Adding to the inability of investors to ascertain key messages from the financial statements is the one-dimensional nature of current financial reporting. All information in the financial statements is presented as if of equal importance. We believe disclosure reform should promote the use of better organization and layering of information in such a way that the presentation of the information itself facilitates improved communication of key messages.

For example, such efficiencies could be attained by highlighting financial statement captions, footnotes, or risks important to investors relative to the current economic environment. Layering of information can be obtained by placing summary information upfront and details following it. Efficiencies can be further obtained by integrating footnotes and placing standing information separately, perhaps as a schedule, to the financial statements.

Other recommendations that would facilitate organization and assist investors include the following:

- *Linking financial statement line items to notes.* Each financial statement line item in both the balance sheet and income statement should be supported by note disclosure.
- *Numbering notes consistently with financial statement presentation.* The numbering sequence of the notes should be driven by the ordering of assets, liabilities, and stockholders' equity in a company's balance sheet, followed by the sequencing of specific income statement and cash flow line items.
- *Reconciling amounts presented in notes to financial statements.* Each balance sheet and income statement amount reported should exactly match the related note disclosure and any supporting schedule provided.
- *Including accounting policies in notes to which they apply.* Accounting policies for specific balance sheet and income statement components should be included with the specific note disclosures.

Improved organization and layering would enhance communication of matters of importance and create greater context so that investors could spend time analyzing results rather than attempting to determine where information is located and which items require their focus. Further, the use of modern technology that allows better drill-down and interactivity of financial statements would also improve delivery of financial reporting information to investors.

9. Simple Language

Disclosure reform should promote the use of simple language. A balanced and candid picture of the business needs to be communicated through commonly understood and well-defined terms. Excessive use of accounting parlance should be minimized because investors are not necessarily familiar with accounting-speak.

10. Tables and Charts

Investors should be provided with the information they need to evaluate their investments in a readily accessible and useful form. To this end, preparers should expand the use of tabular and graphic delivery formats. Users want quantitative tables with entity-specific information appropriately disaggregated. Tabular and other quantitative information should be supported by qualitative explanations that are not littered with boilerplate or generic language. Moreover, standardization of such quantitative disclosures would enhance comparability over time and among firms.

Most Troublesome Disclosures

The most challenging aspects of effective disclosures reside in the following:

- communicating the judgments and estimates made in preparing the financial statements,
- providing a clear and complete picture of economic assets and obligations not included in the financial statements, and
- conveying the risks associated with the business.

During the 2008 financial crisis, it was the undisclosed risks (e.g., subprime risks, liquidity risks), judgments and estimates (e.g., fair values of certain credit derivatives), and off-balance-sheet items (e.g., repos, special purpose entities) that precipitated the problems at many financial institutions. Our 2003 and 2007 Corporate Disclosure Surveys, described in Appendix B, identified many of these areas as the most problematic for investors. Standard setters and regulators need to work to improve disclosures in these areas, and to that end, we include recommendations that address these most troublesome areas.

11. Estimates, Judgments, and Choices

Policy choices, assumptions, judgments, and estimation methods should be clearly disclosed with sufficient detail for investors to understand how they affected the financial results. Furthermore, sensitivity analysis should be required to allow investors an improved understanding of the significance of these underlying estimates and judgments and of the consequences associated with any significant changes.

Every financial statement item—even cash and cash equivalents—incorporates estimates. These estimates are a direct function of managers' assumptions and judgments and affect not only an item's measurement but also whether it is recognized at all. Accordingly, disclosure about these assumptions and judgments is essential if investors are to understand the financial statements and their implications. With sufficient disclosure, investors can make their own assessments about these assumptions and judgments so that, when necessary, they can make changes to reported amounts that reflect their own expectations. More importantly, disclosure permits investors to make better forecasts of future results.

12. Risks

Investors require clear and complete disclosure of a company's risk exposures, its strategies for managing risks, and the effectiveness of those strategies. Further, there should be emphasis and analysis of the most important risks, management's assessment of their likely occurrence, and any potential impact of the risks on amounts presented in the financial statements.

Currently, risk disclosures include a litany of risks that:

- are often generic to the company,
- include no prioritization or emphasis of key risks, and
- do not articulate whether the risks have emerged or whether any connection exists between the risk disclosures and the amounts reflected in the basic financial statements.

Without clear and complete disclosure of a company's risk exposures, its plans and strategies for managing or mitigating those risks, and the effectiveness of its risk management strategies, investors are unable to evaluate the company's potential risks and their impact on future results. The Enhanced Disclosure Task Force of the Financial Stability Board has made useful recommendations with respect to improving risk disclosures by financial institutions, but they are recommendations, not requirements.[45]

13. Off-Balance-Sheet Items

Investors should be given clear and complete disclosure of all off-balance-sheet assets, liabilities, and other financial arrangements and commitments.

The 2008 financial crisis demonstrated to investors that off-balance-sheet vehicles and repurchase transactions can hide leverage and other risks. Although standard setters in the United States have made improvements in the consolidation of off-balance-sheet vehicles, repo agreement accounting has yet to be addressed. The proposed leasing standard that would put leases on the balance sheet is not yet completed and faces resistance.

We believe that all economic assets and obligations that meet our definition of accounting assets and liabilities should be recognized on the balance sheet. No economic assets and liabilities should be omitted from the balance sheet. Until recognition and measurement of all economic assets and liabilities is required, we believe that disclosure should, at a minimum, include summaries of the types of contracts, commitments, and other financial arrangements in which the company has engaged, together with their economic provisions.

Clearly, a need exists for establishing a requirement that focuses disclosures on communicating the substance of all off-balance-sheet transactions and the leverage and risks emanating from such transactions.

14. Commitments and Contingencies

Investors require clear and complete information about a company's contingencies and commitments. Traditionally, financial reporting standards have permitted companies to avoid recognition, measurement, and disclosure of certain arrangements—including executory contracts, commitments, and contingencies—even when an unconditionally binding, definitive agreement exists. Such standards permit managers to structure financial arrangements to avoid recognition or disclosure of material risk exposures until it is beneficial to the company to do so, at settlement, or possibly even permanently. Investors bear the ultimate risk for such exposures. Consequently, they should be fully informed of all such contingencies and risks when they arise.

[45]From "Enhancing the Risk Disclosures of Banks," op. cit.

15. Intangible Assets

Investors require clear and complete information about intangible assets acquired or developed by a company. Intellectual property and other intangible assets are increasingly the economic drivers for many businesses. These assets may be the major sources of a company's revenue generation or contribute significantly to its expense structure. Many, if not most, intangibles, however, are not recognized in the financial statements. But clear and complete information about intangible assets, whether on or off the balance sheet and whether purchased or generated internally, is essential for investors' analyses.

16. Going Concern Issues

Investors require clear and complete information regarding an entity's ability to continue as a going concern. In the CFA Institute Survey on Going Concern (27 March 2012), 61% of respondents indicated that the global financial crisis has highlighted problems with the reporting on going concern. Furthermore, 81% of respondents indicated that the responsibility to report to investors when a question arises as to whether an entity will continue as a going concern lies with the management of the entity. If the conclusion is that the entity may not continue as a going concern, the majority of respondents said the following disclosures should be provided to investors:

- disclosure of risks that directly or indirectly affect the determination that there is a question as to whether the entity is a going concern and
- disclosure of the expected courses of action that bear on the financial flexibility of the entity and a reasonably detailed discussion of the entity's ability to generate sufficient cash to support its operations during at least the 12 months from the date of the financial statements.

17. Go Beyond Requirements if Necessary

To truly explain the economic substance of transactions or events, preparers and auditors should be compelled to provide disclosures that go beyond the requirements in the standards if circumstances warrant. No list of disclosure requirements can comprehensively cover all transactions and events, and disclosure requirements will always lag new types of transactions. Accordingly, included in any disclosure framework should be an overriding principle: Preparers and auditors are obligated to disclose the substance of transactions even if specific requirements do not exist or have not yet been developed.

Furthermore, it is essential that preparers and auditors understand the substance of transactions and go beyond required disclosures related to such transactions or account balances to provide investors with a complete understanding of the underlying economic effects of such transactions. It is not sufficient to merely comply with the rules when information that may be meaningful to investors is not provided.

Considerations to Incorporate in Decisions to Improve Disclosures

The items in this section are matters for standard setters and regulators to consider as they deliberate the improvements needed in disclosures.

18. Materiality

As we noted in Section 7, materiality is an important aspect of disclosure reform and needs to be evaluated closely because investors find that financial statements do not include an obvious amount of immaterial information. In this regard, we recommend the following:

- *Align the definitions of materiality.* Accounting and audit standard setters and regulators need to collaborate to align the definition of materiality found in different pieces of accounting, auditing, and regulatory literature specifically as the definition relates to disclosures.
- *Use an investor perspective in determining materiality.* Materiality thresholds should be established by reference to whether the item or information to be disclosed would make a difference to the decision making of an informed investor. CFA Institute has long argued that investors' information requirements should determine the materiality threshold.
- *Disclose materiality judgments and thresholds.* The materiality judgments exercised by preparers in the preparation of the financial statements should be disclosed in the financial statements. Furthermore, investors would like disclosure of the auditors' materiality thresholds in the auditors' reports. Research demonstrates that, in general, users have a lower materiality threshold than preparers and auditors have. Given the lack of consensus in materiality thresholds between auditors, preparers, and users, such disclosure would provide greater transparency to users and enable them to more readily assess the information presented in the financial statements.

19. Technology

Standard setters and regulators need to look more to the use of technology to facilitate the capture, management, analysis, presentation, and delivery of information to investors. Disclosures broadly, and the disclosure framework specifically, should be developed in the context of advances in technology and connectivity, and they should be responsive to the ever-increasing demand for data. Increased use of technology holds the promise of better (improved quantity and quality of), faster (improved timeliness of), and cheaper (improved access to) information for the user. The SEC should move forward with its 21st Century Disclosure Project.

20. Costs and Benefits

Support for the need to reduce disclosure volume is buoyed by the argument that growing disclosures are increasing the preparers' costs. Often overlooked by those supporting this argument is that it is investors, not preparers, who ultimately bear the cost of such disclosures. The costs to prepare and provide disclosures reduce profits distributable to shareholders. Less information may indeed reduce the length of financial statements and the costs to prepare the statements, but this cost will simply be transferred to investors/shareholders (and is likely to be higher for them).

Accordingly, our view is that any cost–benefit analysis should be done from an investor perspective. It should consider not only the direct cost of producing the disclosures but also the benefit (decreased costs) to investors (generally, multiple investors) of not having to obtain and reprocess this information.

Also missing from cost–benefit analyses is the benefit associated with increased transparency to investors. This aspect clearly should be, but rarely is, evaluated and quantified in the analysis. If necessary disclosures are not provided, investors face significant costs by not having the requisite information to make their investment decisions. The lack of transparency increases the risk premium on debt and equity capital. Improving the quality of disclosures allows for improved capital allocation decisions and lowers the cost of capital. Appendix C cites several academic research papers that demonstrate that transparency through disclosures has the effect of reducing the cost of equity and debt capital.

Disclosure reform should include a more formalized approach to performing cost–benefit analyses. The disclosure framework projects should promote sufficient consideration of the cost to investors of not having the necessary information to make their capital allocation decisions.

21. Behavioral Elements

Financial reporting disclosures are a means of communication by management to investors. All communication is behavioral. The objective of the message, who communicates the message, the method of communication, the nature of the language used, and the timing of the message all determine the message delivered. The recipient determines the message received. All of these aspects are behavioral in origin.

Elements of human behavior may or may not lead to effective communication, and incentives within organizations drive whether disclosures are effective. The postmortems on the Lehman Brothers and MF Global failures and on the JPMorgan Chase London Whale derivatives losses exemplify situations in which incentives and behavior within organizations decreased disclosure transparency.

The FRC's "Louder than Words" report touches on the behavioral aspects of disclosures (see pp. 46–47) and how policymakers can influence behavior through public policy. The EFRAG DP acknowledges (see p. 6) that underlying disclosures is a complex set of behaviors that needs to change. The FASB's disclosure framework document (FASB ITC) does not mention behaviors per se.

Our view is that more work needs to be done by standard setters and regulators to analyze the behavior and incentives behind poor disclosures. Behavior and incentives should then be a consideration in the development of disclosure policy. The 2008 financial crisis and the studies of high-profile failures provide a wealth of information to analyze the disincentives to transparent disclosures.

Considerations Specific to the Development of a Disclosure Framework

We support the development of a disclosure framework. However, as our 2012 Disclosure Survey shows, investors believe other priorities related to improving disclosures should be addressed by standard setters and regulators before they develop a disclosure framework. Improved financial statement presentation and communication and presentational enhancements were considered top priorities in the survey. Furthermore, improvements in the disclosures that proved most troublesome during the 2008 financial crisis are essential to restoring transparency and investor trust. Considerations noted in Exhibit 2, such as materiality, technology, effective cost–benefit analyses, and evaluation of underlying behavioral elements that led to disclosure problems, also should be incorporated in any decision-making process to improve disclosures.

Accordingly, we consider all of the aforementioned recommendations to be elements of disclosure framework development. Set forth in the following sections are several other elements for consideration in the development of a disclosure framework.

22. Focus on Equity Investors

The disclosure framework should be developed with a focus on meeting the information requirements of the equity investor. The primary objective of financial reporting is to meet the information needs of equity investors, creditors, and other suppliers of risk capital so that they can make their resource allocation decisions. Primacy needs to be given to the needs of equity investors, however, because they are the residual risk holders in the enterprise and if their information needs are met, all other suppliers of capital will have the information necessary for their investing or lending decisions.

23. Include Disclosure Objectives

The disclosure framework should promote the inclusion of general disclosure objectives as well as specific disclosure requirements in each standard. The inclusion of disclosure objectives would help ensure that entities provide not only the specifically required disclosures but also information consistent with the spirit or substance of required disclosures or the underlying nature/substance of the transaction. For example, a specific disclosure requirement may necessitate disclosure of short-term borrowings due within the next year, but if the company has short-term borrowings due within the next month that will create liquidity concerns for the entity, the disclosure objective should articulate that such information, although not specifically required, be provided so as to be consistent with the disclosure objective of providing investors with insight into the short-term liquidity of the entity.

24. Maintain Specific Disclosure Standards

The disclosure framework should guide decision making and complement the specific disclosure requirements in individual standards. As noted from the 2012 survey results, investors do not believe the disclosure framework should replace specific disclosure requirements in the individual standards.

Principles alone will not suffice to provide investors with the detailed, disaggregated, and comparable information necessary for their analyses. Thus, disclosure objectives and principles are needed as well as specific disclosure requirements. Specific disclosure requirements are necessary for consistent application of the disclosure requirements by preparers and to ensure a basic degree of comparability, which investors find essential to their analyses. Without specific disclosure requirements, there can be too much flexibility, which can lead to less comparable disclosures.

25. Disclosures Should Be a Focus, Not an Afterthought, in Development of Standards

The disclosure framework should necessitate that standard setters consider the development of disclosures from the outset of the development of accounting standards because disclosures are the means by which the recognition and measurement decisions are communicated to investors.

Presently, disclosures are generally an afterthought to the recognition and measurement phases of accounting standard development. A focus on disclosures would facilitate standard setters themselves better understanding of what the amounts produced by the recognition and measurement elements of the standard will mean and how they should be portrayed/communicated to investors. Failing to improve the disclosures limits the degree to which changes in accounting standards are seen as improvements by investors.

It is important to recognize that the development or existence of a disclosure framework does mean that disclosures are thereby never considered to be an afterthought in the development of accounting standards. The disclosure framework cannot be seen as a substitute for thoughtful disclosure development as accounting standards are created.

26. Comprehensive Information Source

The disclosure framework should ensure that investors have a comprehensive source of audited financial reporting information—the financial statements. The footnotes to the financial statements should not exclude such items as the summary of significant accounting policies or other relevant information that is available from public sources. Excluding such information from the financial statements is likely to raise questions about the boundaries of financial statements and what represents a complete and relevant set of financial statements. Standard setters and regulators need to define what they believe is a comprehensive information set for the financial statements and disregard the notion that other information can be sourced, which would make the financial statements fully meaningful.

27. Applicability

All Entities

The disclosure framework principles should apply to all entities, public and nonpublic. CFA Institute opposes having different financial reporting based on ownership (public, private, not-for-profit[46]), size, or industry. To operate efficiently, capital markets require financial information that is

- comparable from company to company,
- relevant to investment and financing decisions,
- a reliable and faithful depiction of economic reality, and
- neutral.

Permitting alternatives/differences for companies that "do not have public accountability" hinders their analysis. Therefore, we prefer that a disclosure framework apply to both public and nonpublic entities.

All Reporting Periods

The disclosure framework principles should apply to annual and interim reporting. Interim financial statements should provide the same degree of detail and transparency as provided in annual reports. Investors need this information to make informed investment decisions throughout the year. Investment decisions are not made only at year-end.

[46]Please note that there is no well-established definition of nonpublic, or private, company.

Appendix A. Survey Approach and Methods

The position of CFA Institute in support of high-quality disclosures is premised on our mission and member views over a period of several decades (i.e., since at least the 1970s). Our views regarding financial reporting transparency and disclosures were first published in our 1993 publication, "Financial Reporting in the 1990s and Beyond." Our 2007 publication titled *A Comprehensive Business Reporting Model* updated our views on best practices in financial reporting and disclosures.

Over the past several years, CFA Institute has surveyed members regarding many aspects of financial reporting, including disclosures. These surveys provide a way to aggregate member views on matters of importance in financial reporting. The findings contribute to the development and validation of CFA Institute's positions articulated through position papers, responses to standard setters, and other advocacy initiatives. Member support for appropriate transparency and disclosures in financial reporting has been ascertained through these surveys.

Our surveys are completed routinely in the normal course of informing our opinions, not completed specifically to serve any client or commercial interests. We do not pick participants, and our survey reports identify the survey methods, including an unbiased sampling methodology, the response rate, the demographics of participants, and the statistical relevancy of our results. Our interest/survey/commentary is entirely driven by our mission and membership and supported by our advisory committee.

We do not survey our full 100,000 membership on every topic because to do so would be burdensome to our members. We survey those who are most likely to have an interest in or position on (either for or against) a topic. Each member of CFA Institute has a profile that is updated annually with a job classification, and members are asked about areas of interest. On matters of financial reporting, we survey those who have job descriptions relevant to financial reporting (e.g., analyst, portfolio manager) and those who have expressed an interest in financial reporting and financial statement analysis. We also have a more targeted financial reporting survey pool that is a subset of these individuals; it consists of those who have positively expressed interest in being contacted on all our financial reporting matters. To cast as broad, but as relevant, a net as possible on matters of interest, such as financial reporting disclosures, our survey pool on most financial reporting matters generally comprises 15,000 members who are geographically representative of our membership—that is, approximately 52% in the United States and 48% elsewhere.

For the 2012 Disclosure Survey, we sent an e-mail invitation, with a link to the web-based survey, to 14,041 members in February 2012. The survey questionnaire consisted of 12 questions. We received 332 valid responses, for an overall response rate of 2.4%. The margin of error (based on the sampling population) is ±5.37% at the 95% confidence level. The margin of error is based on the size of the target population and the number of responses received (not the actual response rate); with 332 responses, we can be 95% confident that the reported percentage (i.e., results) includes the "true" percentage within 5 percentage points above or below the reported percentage. Each question had a "no opinion" option, which has been excluded from the calculations displayed in each figure; accordingly, the margin of error varies by question depending on the number of respondents.

The response rate we received on the survey questions discussed in this report is statistically relevant and consistent with other surveys in both number of participants and response rate.

Tables A1–A6 present a summary of the geographical, occupational, and experience statistics of respondents to the survey.

Table A1. **Respondents by Geographical Area**

Region	Invited	Responded	Response Rate
Americas	9,377	203	2%
Asia Pacific	2,088	62	3%
Europe, Middle East and Africa	2,576	67	3%
Total	**14,041**	**332**	

Table A2. **Respondents by Country**

Country	Invited	Responded	Response Rate
United States	7,800	171	2%
Canada	1,376	23	2%
United Kingdom	1,119	16	1%
Hong Kong	486	4	1%
China	350	14	4%
Singapore	311	10	3%
Australia	275	6	2%

(continued)

Table A2. Respondents by Country (continued)

Country	Invited	Responded	Response Rate
Germany	235	7	3%
Switzerland	229	7	3%
India	182	9	5%
South Africa	179	5	3%
United Arab Emirates	8	1	13%
Other	1,491	59	4%
Total	**14,041**	**332**	

Table A3. Respondents by Occupation

Occupation	Invited	Responded	Response Rate
Research analyst	7,015	139	2%
Portfolio manager	6,663	160	2%
Other	241	33	14%
Total	**14,041**	**332**	

Table A4. Respondents by Years in Industry

Years in Industry	Invited	Responded	Response Rate
5 years or less	966	41	4%
6–10 years	3,967	97	2%
11–15 years	3,875	65	2%
16–20 years	2,481	52	2%
More than 20 years	2,663	41	2%
Not provided*	89	3	3%
Total	**14,041**	**332**	

*Information not provided by respondent.

Table A5. Respondents by Type of Asset Base

Asset Base	Invited	Responded	Response Rate
Institutional	5,753	113	2%
Private	3,153	90	3%
Both	2,117	31	1%
Not provided*	3,018	90	3%
Total	**14,041**	**332**	

*Information not provided by respondent.

Table A6. Respondents by Primary Investment Practice

Primary Investment Practice	Invited	Responded	Response Rate
Equities	8,831	176	2%
Fixed income	2,753	70	3%
Private equity	461	14	3%
Hedge funds	310	10	3%
Real estate	214	9	4%
Structured products	140	9	6%
Derivatives	133	7	5%
Commodities	71	3	4%
Indexed	64	3	5%
Venture capital	58	3	5%
Foreign currency	37	0	0%
Other	293	10	3%
Not provided*	676	25	4%
Total	**14,041**	**332**	

*Information not provided by respondent.

Appendix B. Prior CFA Institute Survey Results

CFA Institute has conducted multiple surveys over the last decade on financial reporting issues of interest to our members. Provided here are details of two prior surveys and their key findings. The themes that emerged from these surveys are consistent with the 2012 Disclosure Survey results.

Corporate Disclosure Surveys

2003 Corporate Disclosure Survey

CFA Institute surveyed members in 2003 to obtain feedback on the following:

- the importance of certain financial information to members' analyses and comparison of companies' financial performance and investment potential;
- whether corporate disclosures met their needs; and
- if not, what additional information is needed and/or how it should be presented.

The survey covered a wide range of financial reporting elements—to name a few, financial statement presentation choices, cash flow statement choices, segment reporting, and disclosures provided with financial statements.

2007 Corporate Disclosure Survey

We updated and expanded the 2003 Corporate Disclosure Survey, conducting the survey again in 2007. The 2007 Corporate Disclosure Survey updated certain questions asked in 2003 and asked more detailed questions in other areas.

Key Survey Findings

The results of the surveys are consistent in finding a need for information in disclosures that is of high quality and is sufficient for financial statement analysis and investment decision making. The surveys also provide indications of the disclosures that investors rank of highest importance but that are in need of greatest improvement (i.e., where members find disclosures to be overly aggregated, lacking in quality, or inclusive of gaps in information content).

Need for Sufficient Disclosure

If investors are to understand the amounts reported in the financial statements, they need to have sufficient supplementary disclosures to evaluate the numbers. These disclosures may include

- financial reporting methods used,
- models used for estimation and measurement,
- assumptions used,
- sensitivity analysis of point estimates,
- information about risk exposures, and
- information explaining why changes in important items have occurred.

Need for Quality Information

The importance rating of periodic financial reports in the 2003 and 2007 surveys consistently shows that annual reports (e.g., SEC Form 10-Ks) rank as the most important report. The implication is that the depth and quality of financial information contained in a report has a higher weighting than the frequency of its issuance. The following list contains examples of disclosures for which investors have desired improvements in quality:

- *Off-balance-sheet disclosures.* In the surveys, off-balance-sheet disclosures had the widest gap between importance of the item and quality of information provided; that is, the disclosures were high in importance and low in quality. From a review of the respondents' comments, we glean that they believed that companies in general do not provide enough transparent disclosure with regard to off-balance-sheet arrangements.

- *Nonfinancial and forward-looking information.* Disclosures about nonfinancial information and forward-looking information ranked next highest in importance after disclosures of off-balance-sheet assets and liabilities. Respondents indicated that these disclosures had significant gaps in quality.

- *Fair value.* Investors ranked fair value disclosures high in importance in both surveys. They also reported gaps in the quality of information provided.

- *Accounting estimates.* Disclosures relating to accounting estimates and reserves, including key assumptions and sensitivity analyses, ranked high in importance and low in quality of information provided. Respondents indicated that more-detailed information regarding assumptions, sensitivity analyses, and judgments used in estimating reserves is needed for the disclosures to be useful.

- *Derivatives, hedging, and contingencies.* Disclosures regarding derivatives and hedging activities, risks, and the company's exposures to risks and contingencies related to litigation and potential exposure ranked high in importance. Each of these areas also showed gaps in the quality of information provided.

- *Cash flows.* With regard to cash flow disclosures, most respondents attached the highest importance and perceived the largest gap in information for note disclosures about contractual or future cash outflows. This area was followed by the disclosures of operating cash flows. This finding indicates a need for improved cash flow disclosures in the footnotes and the creation of a direct cash flow statement.

- *Extraordinary, unusual, and nonrecurring charges.* Disclosures relating to extraordinary, unusual, or nonrecurring charges were ranked high in importance but low in quality of information provided. Respondents indicated that the data are too aggregated to be meaningful.

Need for Greater Disclosure in Audit Reports

Investors responding to the 2003 and 2007 surveys desired a more detailed independent auditor report that would disclose amounts or changes in amounts that have a high degree of uncertainty in measurement, that involve significant assumptions, and so on. In addition, they believed the auditor's report should include assessments of materiality and disclosures about changes in accounting principles affecting the consistency of reported amounts. These disclosures would allow investors to better analyze these matters and make changes to their own analyses and models.

Appendix C. Academic Research: Greater Transparency = Lower Cost of Capital

In support of our call for high-quality comprehensive disclosures, we cite in this appendix several studies (by no means all) concluding that increased disclosure provides investors with greater transparency into their holdings, which results in a decrease in the cost of equity capital, public debt, and private debt capital and thus increases equity values.[47] Moreover, one study cited demonstrates that the cost of equity capital is reduced most significantly as a product of both strong shareholder rights and a high degree of financial disclosure. The abstracts are from the originals.

"Relationship between Cost of Equity Capital and Voluntary Corporate Disclosures."

Petrova, Elena, Georgios Georgakopoulos, Ioannis Sotiropoulos, and Konstantinos Z. Vasileio. *International Journal of Economics and Finance*, vol. 4, no. 3 (March 2012):83.

"Economic theory suggests that by increasing the level of corporate reporting firms not only increase their stock market liquidity, but they also decrease the investors' estimation risk, arising from uncertainty about future returns and payout distributions. Utilizing the Residual Income Valuation Model, the implied cost of capital is estimated for a sample of 121 Swiss listed, non-financial companies adopting a finite horizon version of the residual income valuation model. The results show that firms on the Swiss market can reduce their cost of equity capital by increasing the level of their voluntary corporate disclosures. The results persist even after controlling for various firm specific factors, such as size and financial leverage, and regardless of the company's reporting strategy (conservative or aggressive)."

[47]FASB's Business Reporting Research Project: In 2001, the Business Reporting Research Project sponsored by the FASB published its report titled "Improving Business Reporting: Insights into Enhancing Voluntary Disclosures." The objective of the report was to help companies improve their business reporting by providing evidence that many leading companies are making extensive voluntary disclosures and by listing examples of those disclosures. The examples serve to provide companies with helpful ideas of how to describe and explain their investment potential to investors. The basic premise underlying this Business Reporting Research Project was that improving disclosures makes the capital allocation process more efficient and reduces the average cost of capital.

"Corporate Disclosure Quality and the Cost of Debt."

Partha Sengupta. *Accounting Review*, vol. 73, no. 4 (October 1998):459.

"This paper provides evidence that firms with high disclosure quality ratings from financial analysts enjoy a lower effective interest cost of issuing debt. This finding is consistent with the argument that a policy of timely and detailed disclosures reduces lenders' and underwriters' perception of default risk of the disclosing firm, reducing its cost of debt. The results also indicate that the relative importance of disclosures is greater in situations where there is greater market uncertainty about the firm as reflected by the variance of stock returns. Since debt financing is an important part of external financing for publicly traded firms, the results have important implications on our understanding of the motives and consequences of public disclosures."

"Disclosure and the Loan Spread on Private Debt."

Simon C. Mazumdar and Partha Sengupta. *Financial Analysts Journal*, vol. 61, no. 3 (May/June 2005):83.

"Companies that consistently make detailed, timely, and informative disclosures face lower costs of public equity and debt capital. The study reported here investigated whether such companies also face lower interest costs on private debt contracts. Examination of a sample of 173 new private debt issues during the 1989–93 period suggests that, after company- and loan-specific factors and market conditions have been controlled for, loan spreads are negatively associated with a measure of companies' overall disclosure quality. That is, companies with consistently high ratings for voluntary disclosures pay lower interest on their private debt (bank loan) contracts."

"Disclosure Incentives and Effects on Cost of Capital around the World."

Jere R. Francis, Inder K. Khurana, and Raynolde Pereira. *Accounting Review*, vol. 80, no. 4 (October 2005):1125.

"Prior research predicts that firms reliant on external financing are more likely to undertake a higher level of disclosure, and a higher disclosure level should, in turn, lead to a lower cost of external financing. This paper tests these predictions outside the United States where alternative legal and financial systems could mitigate the effectiveness of such disclosures and, comprehensively, examines both disclosure incentives and disclosure consequences on cost of capital for a common set of firms. Using a sample from 34 countries, we find that firms in industries with greater external financing needs have higher voluntary disclosure levels, and that an expanded disclosure policy for these firms leads to a lower cost of both debt and equity capital. Cross-country differences in legal and financial systems affect observed disclosure levels in predicted ways. However, a surprising result in the study is that voluntary disclosure incentives appear to operate independently of country-level factors, which suggests the effectiveness of voluntary disclosure in gaining access to lower cost external financing around the world."

"Shareholder Rights, Financial Disclosure and the Cost of Equity Capital."

C.S. Agnes Cheng, Denton Collins, and Henry He Huang. *Review of Quantitative Finance and Accounting*, vol. 27, no. 2 (September 2006):175.

"Using cost-of-equity-capital estimates derived from expected earnings growth valuation models, we find that firms with stronger shareholder rights regimes and higher levels of financial transparency are associated with significantly lower costs of equity capital. We also find evidence that greater financial disclosure and stronger rights regimes interact in reducing firms' costs of equity capital, such that the effect of a high level of one mechanism is minimal when it is combined with a low level of the other. Finally, we document that neither factor dominates the other in their associations, and that there are tradeoffs between disclosure levels and shareholder rights in their influence on firms' implied costs of equity capital."

CFA Institute

AUTHORS

Mohini Singh, ACA
Director
Financial Reporting Policy

Sandra J. Peters, CPA, CFA
Head
Financial Reporting Policy

CONTRIBUTOR

Kurt Schacht, JD, CFA
Managing Director
Standards and Financial
Market Integrity

Made in United States
Cleveland, OH
05 November 2026

47649283R00071